101 TIPS
FOR SCORING HIGH
ON THE
GMAT

Thomas H. Martinson

ARCO PUBLISHING, INC.
NEW YORK

One for Stephen

Published by Arco Publishing, Inc.
215 Park Avenue South, New York, NY 10003

Copyright © 1985 by Thomas H. Martinson

All rights reserved. No part of this book may
be reproduced, by any means, without permission
in writing from the publisher, except by a
reviewer who wishes to quote brief excerpts in
connection with a review in a magazine or
newspaper.

Library of Congress Cataloging in Publication Data

Martinson, Thomas H.
 101 tips for scoring high on the GMAT.

 1. Management—Examinations, questions, etc.
2. Business—Examinations, questions, etc.   I. Title.
II. Title: One hundred one tips for scoring high on
the GMAT.
HD30.413.M37   1985   650'.076   85-1433
ISBN 0-668-05727-0 (Paper Edition)

Printed in the United States of America

CONTENTS

A Note to the Reader iv

Chapter 1:   Basics 1

Chapter 2:   Problem Solving 13

Chapter 3:   Data Sufficiency 57

Chapter 4:   Analysis of Situations 91

Chapter 5:   Reading Comprehension 121

Chapter 6:   Sentence Correction 144

A NOTE TO THE READER

The Graduate Management Admission Test (GMAT) is a standardized test prepared by Educational Testing Service (ETS) for the Graduate Management Admission Council, an association of representatives from graduate schools of management. Most graduate schools of management require applicants to take the GMAT as part of the admissions process. To register to take the test, write to:

> Graduate Management Admission Test
> Educational Testing Service
> Box 966-R
> Princeton, N.J. 08541

The exact weight given to the GMAT score varies from school to school. Some schools have very rigid standards and rarely, if ever, accept an applicant with a GMAT score below a certain minimum level. Other schools are more flexible, discounting the importance of the GMAT if other factors favor acceptance. Still, no matter how impressive the other aspects of an applicant's profile, an unsatisfactory GMAT score will almost always mean rejection. At schools where the competition for admission is very keen, even an adequate GMAT score may not be sufficient for acceptance. You can't afford not to prepare for this test.

In this book, we review every area that has been officially announced for use on the GMAT:

- Problem Solving
- Data Sufficiency
- Analysis of Situations
- Reading Comprehension
- Sentence Correction

We subject each of the substantive areas to a rigorous analysis, dissecting the question types to show you how they are constructed and what the test writers are looking for. We include numerous suggestions for improving your scores, presented in easy-to-remember keys. The points made in this book are illustrated by numerous examples.

One of the most important features of this book is that it tells you things the exam preparers do not tell you. For example, we identify certain patterns to the incorrect choices which are not mentioned in the official materials distributed by the exam preparers. We emphasize alternative attack strategies that exploit the test structure, strategies that the exam preparers simply do not discuss in their materials.

This book is entirely self-contained. If, however, after studying this material, you believe that you would benefit from further practice for the exam, we recommend that you obtain a copy of the Arco practice manual for the GMAT. You will find the practice materials included in that book provide valuable reinforcement of the points discussed in this book.

1.
BASICS

If you have already taken the Graduate Management Admission Test (GMAT), or other, similar exams, then some of this information will be familiar to you. Do not, however, skip this chapter. Use it to refamiliarize yourself with the fundamentals of standardized test taking and to learn how the GMAT is different from other tests you have taken: for example, is there a penalty for incorrect responses? If you have never taken an exam like the GMAT, or had taken such a test a long time ago, you will want to read this chapter carefully. And when you register to take the exam, you should read *GMAT: Bulletin of Information*, a pamphlet made available free of charge by the Graduate Management Admission Council. It contains test registration materials and includes the answers to many specialized questions about services such as emergency score reporting, topics that do not come within the scope of this book.

TOPICS COVERED ON THE GMAT

The GMAT comprises five topics divided into the general areas of math skills and verbal skills. The math area includes problem solving and data sufficiency. The verbal area includes reading comprehension, sentence correction, and analysis of situations.

THE FORMAT OF THE GMAT

The GMAT consists of eight separately timed sections, each with a time limit of 30 minutes. During the test, you are allowed to work only on the particular section that is being timed. You may not go back to sections that were previously completed, nor are you permitted to skip ahead. The exam proctor announces when time for work on a section begins and when it ends.

The number of questions in a section varies according to the topic being tested:

Topic	Number of Questions
Problem Solving	20
Data Sufficiency	25
Reading Comprehension	25
Sentence Correction	25
Analysis of Situations	35

The distribution and order of sections varies from administration to administration. You can, however, count on seeing two problem-solving sections plus one each of the remaining topics. That makes a total of six sections. The topics for the other two sections are chosen by the test developers, but these two extra sections are not used to compute your GMAT score. Instead, the two extra sections are used for developing new questions. These two extra sections, containing questions still in the developmental phase, may appear at any point during the test and will probably not be recognizably different from other sections. A sample test format:

Topic	Number of Questions Scored
Section 1: Reading Comprehension	25
Section 2: Analysis of Situations (Developmental)	0
Section 3: Problem Solving	20
Section 4: Data Sufficiency	25
Section 5: Sentence Correction	25
Section 6: Analysis of Situations	35
Section 7: Problem Solving (Developmental)	0
Section 8: Problem Solving	20
Total Questions Scored	150

Administration of the entire test takes anywhere from $4\frac{1}{2}$ to 5 hours. Some time is used before the actual exam begins for seating candidates in the testing rooms, checking identification, distributing materials, filling out information sheets, and at the end in collecting test booklets and answer sheets.

At some point during the test, the proctor will give you a 10- to 15-minute break. Aside from that break, however, the sections follow each other without interruption.

SCORING THE GMAT

You enter your answers to questions on an answer sheet by blackening appropriate spaces. This answer sheet is machine graded, and a computer generates your GMAT scores. Your score report will include three scores: a math subscore based on the two problem-solving sections with the data-sufficiency section; a verbal subscore based on the reading comprehension, sentence correction, and analysis of situations sections; and a composite score based on the six "live" sections.

The reported scores are based upon what is called the corrected raw score. The corrected raw score is computed as follows:

$$\text{Number of Correct Answers} - \frac{1}{4}(\text{Number of Incorrect Answers}) = \text{Corrected Raw Score}$$

For example, if you attempt 120 questions out of the 150 on the test, answering 100 correctly and missing 20, your corrected raw score would be:

$$100 - \frac{1}{4}(20) = 95$$

This corrected raw score is then converted to the scaled or reported scores according to tables developed by ETS. The math and verbal subscores are reported on scales ranging from 0 to 60, while the composite score is reported on a scale ranging from 200 to 800. The reported scores are also matched to percentile equivalents. Here are some sample conversions:

| Composite Score ||| Math Subscore ||| Verbal Subscore |||
Raw Score	Scaled Score	Percentile Equivalent	Raw Score	Scaled Score	Percentile Equivalent	Raw Score	Scaled Score	Percentile Equivalent
150	800	99	65		99	85	53	99
140	790	99	55	49	99	75	47	99
130	760	99	45	42	95	65	41	94
120	710	99	35	35	78	55	34	77
100	620	93	25	28	55	45	28	53
90	590	87	20	24	36	40	25	40
80	530	70						
70	480	53						
60	440	38						

Source: *The Official Guide to GMAT* (Graduate Management Admission Council 1982), pp. 188–89.

HOW SCORES ARE USED

An extended discussion on how to apply to business school is outside the scope of this book, but we can offer one or two generalizations about the use schools make of the scores. First, by far the most important of the three scores is the composite score. It is this score that many schools use in screening applications. The subscores are more often used to advise students who are accepted. For example, if a school emphasizing quantitative methods accepts a student with a low math subscore, the school may advise that student to take an additional math course before enrolling.

Second, many schools set minimum GMAT scores below which they do not accept applicants. Methods of doing this vary from school to school. Some schools simply announce that applicants should have a certain minimum score, say 450. Others use a mathematical formula to combine the GMAT score and the undergraduate grade point average. For example:

$$GMAT + (200 \times GPA) = Total$$

Thus a student with a GMAT score of 450 and a GPA of 3.0 would have a formula total of 1050. A school may set a minimum total on this formula below which it will not accept an applicant.

Before you submit an application, you should read the descriptive catalogue provided by the school to determine whether you are competitive for that school. There is no reason to waste time and money applying to a school that requires a GMAT score or a grade point average (GPA) substantially above what you have.

GENERAL METHODS OF ATTACK

Preview

Since some slight variations in test format, including the number of questions in a section, are possible,

| Before beginning work on a section, preview the section. |

To preview the section, take 10 seconds or so and flip through the pages of that section. The preview will alert you to any changes in the test format and allow you to adjust your strategy accordingly. Additionally, during the preview, you will have an opportunity to recall the important keys for that section. Seeing a familiar geometry figure or question stem will help you focus attention on the type of question you are attacking.

For the same reasons, you should include in your preview a glance at the instructions. You should not, however, stop to reread them carefully:

Be familiar with the instructions for each question type *before* the exam. On the exam, give the instructions a cursory check, but *do not reread the instructions*.

No additional time is given during a section for reading the directions. If you already know the directions, a quick check of no more than 5 seconds will refresh your memory, and that is all that is required.

Pacing

No testing technique is more important than pacing. The computer that grades your test understands only the simple formula:

$$\text{Correct} - \frac{1}{4}(\text{Incorrect}) = \text{Corrected Raw Score}.$$

No points are awarded for near misses, and no bonuses are given for accuracy.

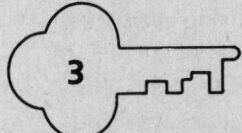

Find the best compromise between speed and accuracy.

On the one hand, you cannot afford to be sloppy. Not only do you get no credit for an incorrect response, but you lose a fraction of a point for a tried but missed question. On the other hand, you cannot afford to be so careful that you do not get adequate coverage. Somewhere there is an ideal point of compromise between speed and accuracy, and this is different for different people.

To dramatize the importance of finding this best compromise, consider the cases of three test takers. Peter Goodstudent, Paul Haphazard, and Mary Testwise. On a certain GMAT, of the "live" 150 questions, Peter attempted only 60, but he was very accurate, missing only 4 questions. Paul worked very quickly, too quickly, attempting all 150 questions, missing 80 of them—over half. Mary attempted 120 questions, and she missed 32. Their score reports would show:

Peter:
Corrected Raw Score = $56 - \frac{1}{4}(4)$ = 55/Scaled Score: 410/Percentile: 29

Paul:
Corrected Raw Score = $70 - \frac{1}{4}(80)$ = 50/Scaled Score: 390/Percentile: 25

Mary:
Corrected Raw Score = $88 - \frac{1}{4}(32)$ = 80/Scaled Score: 570/Percentile: 83

The allegorical names tell the story.
The corollary to Key 3 is this:

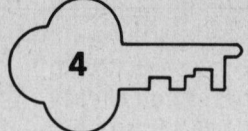

> If, after a reasonable time, a solution is not forthcoming, leave the question.

All questions are given equal weight. No extra credit is given for difficult questions. So you cannot afford to keep working on a question after you have made a reasonable, but unsuccessful, attempt. Rather, you should leave it and keep working through the section.

Key 4 advises you to *leave* a question after making a reasonable attempt at a solution; it does not advise that you completely skip a question because the question appears to be difficult.

> Do not automatically skip a question just because it looks as if the question will require some work.

Most of the questions on the exam do require analysis; and if you skip every question that looks as if it will require work, you will quickly find yourself at the end of the section, having answered no questions at all.

Time Management

Time management is related to pacing, but the two are not the same. Time management means keeping track of the passing minutes and using each minute as fully as possible.

> Bring a watch and set it for "test time."

The proctor in charge of administering the exam will announce when work is to begin on a section and when it is to end, and usually the proctors will announce the passing time by writing the remaining time on a chalkboard. But the proctor may not write "10 minutes remaining" on the chalkboard at exactly the 10-minute mark. Or you may not see the proctor enter the note. As a result, when you first see "10 minutes remaining," you may have anywhere from 10 minutes to no time at all to complete the section.

With your watch you will know exactly how much time remains. If your watch has a stopwatch function, use it. If you have an analog watch (one with hands), set the time to "test time." At the beginning of each section, set your watch to 11:30. The section will then be over at exactly 12:00.

Not only must you be aware of the passing of time, you must also use that time to good advantage:

Avoid letting your mind wander. If you must pause during a section, do so as a matter of choice, and only for a predetermined time.

Since you cannot expect unbroken concentration for the entire time period, learn to recognize the signs of mental fatigue and have a plan for resting when you must. If you find your mind wandering or if you find that you are reading the same line over and over without comprehension, then pause for a few seconds. When you determine that a break is needed, put down your pencil, close your eyes, and relax by rubbing your temples or by means of some other soothing exercise, for a predetermined time, say 15 seconds. Then get back to work.

While it is important to monitor the passing of time, it is equally imperative that time management not become a morbid obsession.

Do not become preoccupied with the passing time.

There are convenient points in each section at which it is natural to check the time. For example, in the math sections, a page contains only four or five questions. Work the first page of questions, then consult your watch. After that, check your watch every few questions.

Take Advantage of the Test Structure

One of the most important design features of a test like the GMAT is that the correct answer to the question is actually given, hidden in a group of four similar but incorrect choices. In this book, we develop techniques to help you distinguish the correct choice from its camouflage background. Generally,

Eliminate any choice that cannot possibly be the correct answer to the question asked.

Consider the following reading comprehension question:

The author's conclusion about the status of health in the United States is supported by evidence that is

(A) hypothetical
(B) social
(C) fragmented
(D) biased
(E) empirical

Even without the reading passage on which this question is based, it is possible to eliminate three of the five choices. (A) can be eliminated because the idea of hypothetical evidence is self-contradictory. (B) can be eliminated because it makes no sense to say "The author's evidence for this conclusion is social." (C) can be eliminated on the same ground: what would it mean to be "fragmented evidence." Both (D) and (E) appear to be plausible answers. Evidence can be empirical, but it can also be biased. Even though we cannot finally choose either (D) or (E), we can eliminate three of the five choices on the grounds that they simply are not possible answers to the question asked.

This brings us to the question of guessing:

Never guess blindly. Always guess when you are able to eliminate one or more choices.

The so-called "penalty" is designed to eliminate any advantage to random guessing. This can be shown by setting up a situation in which a person guesses blindly at, say, 100 questions. Since there are five choices to pick from, the person should hit on the right answer in one out of every five questions. Thus, he or she should answer correctly, by guessing, $\frac{1}{5}$ of the 100 questions, missing the remaining 80. The corrected raw score would be:

$$20 - \frac{1}{4}(80) = 20 - 20 = 0$$

Theoretically, over a large enough pool of questions, the net result from guessing blindly should be zero.

The situation is very different when you are able to eliminate even one answer choice. Given a pool of 100 questions, if you are able to eliminate even one choice to each question, your corrected raw score should be:

$$25 - \frac{1}{4}(75) = 6.25$$

a net gain. The results are even more favorable when you can eliminate two or more choices; and this may be possible, as we have shown with the preceding reading comprehension question.

You must realize that when you are guessing, you are doing just that.

When the time comes to guess, guess quickly and do not change your mind.

When it is time to guess, go ahead and get it over with. You are guessing because you have exhausted your analytical resources. There is no reason to prefer one choice over another, so make your guess. There is some evidence that first guesses are more likely to be correct than second guesses. Perhaps the reason for this is that a hunch represents a partially formed analytical judgment. Thus, the guess is actually more than a guess. If this is true, it is better not to change your first guess.

There is one more point about answer patterns. A string of four or five is theoretically possible, and given the large number of tests developed by ETS, we should have seen such strings. That we have not suggests that the test writers limit the length of strings:

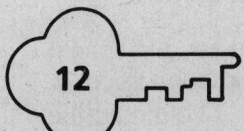

Strings of three are acceptable. Strings of four or more should be broken.

If you find a string of four or more in your answers, check your work. At least one of the four is incorrect.

Answer Sheet Management

The test materials consist of two parts: a booklet containing the questions and a separate answer sheet with groups of lettered spaces for coding your responses to questions in the booklet:

10 / 101 Tips for Scoring High on the GMAT

1 Ⓐ Ⓑ Ⓒ Ⓓ Ⓔ	6 Ⓐ Ⓑ Ⓒ Ⓓ Ⓔ	11 Ⓐ Ⓑ Ⓒ Ⓓ Ⓔ	16 Ⓐ Ⓑ Ⓒ Ⓓ Ⓔ	21 Ⓐ Ⓑ Ⓒ Ⓓ Ⓔ
2 Ⓐ Ⓑ Ⓒ Ⓓ Ⓔ	7 Ⓐ Ⓑ Ⓒ Ⓓ Ⓔ	12 Ⓐ Ⓑ Ⓒ Ⓓ Ⓔ	17 Ⓐ Ⓑ Ⓒ Ⓓ Ⓔ	22 Ⓐ Ⓑ Ⓒ Ⓓ Ⓔ
3 Ⓐ Ⓑ Ⓒ Ⓓ Ⓔ	8 Ⓐ Ⓑ Ⓒ Ⓓ Ⓔ	13 Ⓐ Ⓑ Ⓒ Ⓓ Ⓔ	18 Ⓐ Ⓑ Ⓒ Ⓓ Ⓔ	23 Ⓐ Ⓑ Ⓒ Ⓓ Ⓔ
4 Ⓐ Ⓑ Ⓒ Ⓓ Ⓔ	9 Ⓐ Ⓑ Ⓒ Ⓓ Ⓔ	14 Ⓐ Ⓑ Ⓒ Ⓓ Ⓔ	19 Ⓐ Ⓑ Ⓒ Ⓓ Ⓔ	24 Ⓐ Ⓑ Ⓒ Ⓓ Ⓔ
5 Ⓐ Ⓑ Ⓒ Ⓓ Ⓔ	10 Ⓐ Ⓑ Ⓒ Ⓓ Ⓔ	15 Ⓐ Ⓑ Ⓒ Ⓓ Ⓔ	20 Ⓐ Ⓑ Ⓒ Ⓓ Ⓔ	25 Ⓐ Ⓑ Ⓒ Ⓓ Ⓔ

Be sure to code your responses on the answer sheet completely, darkly, and neatly. Avoid stray marks that could be misread by the machine. Enter only one answer to each question. Do not worry if the answer sheet contains more spaces than there are questions in your test booklet. Leave them blank.

Key 13 is most easily explained visually:

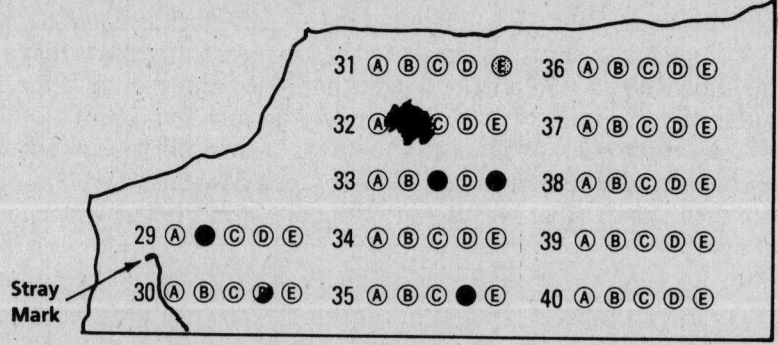

The answers to questions 29 and 35 are correctly entered. The mark for question 30 is incomplete and may not be picked up by the machine. The mark for question 31 is too light; again, the machine may miss it. The mark for question 32 is messy; the machine could read (A), (B), and (C). Question 33 will be graded as incorrect since there are two choices coded. Question 34 is blank. Omissions are neither wrong nor right; they do not affect the score. Assuming the section contained exactly 35 questions, the spaces for answers to questions 36 through 40 have been correctly left empty. The stray mark should be erased.

The most serious of all answer-sheet management errors is coding out of sequence. An error of sequence occurs when a candidate skips a question and fails to skip the corresponding space on the answer sheet, or vice versa. The result is a correct pattern of choices that is displaced by one or more questions on the answer sheet. The machine is unforgiving of this error. It reads them as intended but incorrect responses. To minimize the danger of a sequence error:

Code your answer sheets in blocks.

Most examinees make the mistake of transcribing answers one by one. It is more efficient to code your answer sheet in groups. Wait until you have solved five or six questions and then enter your responses to those questions on your answer sheet. This cuts down on the paper shuffling, and it also reduces the chance of a sequence error. You will find convenient points at which to stop to perform this bookkeeping chore; for example, you can do this as you are ready to turn the page of your test booklet. You can also use the coding time as a break period. When you feel the need for a short break, quit thinking and do something mindless such as catching up your answer sheet. As time in the section winds down, you should go to the one-by-one coding method. You do not want time to run out before you have had a chance to code all of your responses.

We recommend you keep a separate record of all your answers:

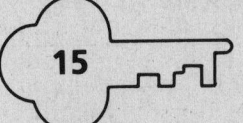

Develop a record-keeping system for use in the test booklet.

One part of the system should be a device for noting the correct answer. The system should also have a device for noting when you have made a change in your answer. There should also be a way of noting which questions you have skipped and of signaling questions that you want to recheck if time permits. There is no single, uniquely correct system for record keeping. You may want to use some of the following devices:

Correct Answer: Circle letter.
Definitely Eliminate Choice: "x" over letter.
Changed Choice: Fill in circle of previous choice, and circle new choice.
Skipped Question: "?" by number of question.
Question to Recheck: Circle number of question.

Such a system will enable you to keep track of what remains to be done. Additionally, should you discover you have made an error on your answer sheet, the system will allow you to retrieve your work in a fairly short period of time.

PERFORMANCE EXPECTATIONS

The GMAT differs in many respects from the teacher-prepared exams you took in college, so you must adjust your performance expectations accordingly. First:

The GMAT includes some very difficult questions.

You must realize that the population taking the GMAT is not representative of the population as a whole. Business school candidates are not only people who have finished or who are about to finish college, they are people who have been reasonably successful in school, in business, or in both. The very fact that someone is taking the GMAT is evidence that that person believes she or he is a pretty good thinker and has a chance of getting into business school, a pretty competitive undertaking. To create a test that will distinguish the very best from a group of the best, the test writers must include some very difficult questions.

Not only are some of the questions very difficult, you are not given a lot of time to do them:

You are likely to experience severe time pressure on the exam.

In college, you probably had enough time to handle all or at least most of the questions on your exams. The GMAT is different. You will run out of time, not once, but eight different times. The time pressure accentuates the difficulty of the questions.

Third, the scoring mechanism for the GMAT is different from those of teacher-prepared tests. Most college tests are graded on the traditional 100-point scale, with 90+ being an A, 80 to 89 being a B, etc. Most students expect to answer in excess of 75 or 80 percent of the questions on a teacher-prepared exam, but:

You cannot expect to answer correctly 75 to 80 percent of the questions on the GMAT.

Answering correctly 80 percent of the 150 questions (and for the purpose of simplicity assuming no incorrect responses), a student would have a corrected raw score of 120, a composite score of 710, and a percentile ranking of 99+. A corrected raw score of 112, about 75 percent of 150, would generate a composite score of 680 and a percentile ranking of 98 percent. So very few people answer 75 or 80 percent of the questions correctly.

In fact, a corrected raw score of only half the possible total of 150, or 75, generates a scaled score of 510 and a percentile ranking of 64—well above an average score. You must, therefore, adjust your expectations to fit the GMAT.

To adjust your expectations does not mean, however, settling for a GMAT score below what you want. This book will assist you in preparing for the GMAT, and we hope that it will assist you in achieving your desired GMAT score.

2. PROBLEM SOLVING

THE TYPES OF QUESTIONS

Mention the words "math exam" and we think of questions on some special topic of algebra or geometry, such as factoring or right triangles. This is natural since we were taught and tested on math as a series of different subjects. Arithmetic was broken down into addition, division, fractions, decimals, and so on. Algebra was presented in stages such as manipulating letters, factoring expressions, and solving equations. We learned the important principles of geometry by studying the features of the various figures such as triangles, squares, and circles. Most mathematics review texts tend to respect these traditional divisions, but a math review is only the beginning of your preparation for the Graduate Management Admission Test (GMAT). The authors of the exam are not constrained to write questions that can be easily classified as "factoring" or "Pythagorean formula." Of course, the questions in this section presuppose a knowledge of the fundamental principles of math, but questions are developed according to a set of guidelines specifically designed for the GMAT. Consequently, the exam writers operate within a framework that is related to the traditional approach to math, but different from it in very important respects. So you must learn to see a GMAT question in this section through the eyes of the test writer.

The three types of questions studied in this chapter are:

1. Manipulation problems
2. Practical word problems
3. Geometry problems

Manipulation Problems

A manipulation question is an item that tests ability to perform some basic operation in arithmetic or algebra.

Question 2-1

0.5 × 0.002 =

(A) 0.0001 (B) 0.001 (C) 0.01 (D) 0.1 (E) 1.0

A quick calculation (making sure you keep track of the number of decimal places) shows that the correct answer is (B), and you may wonder whether such an easy question would actually appear on the GMAT. Such an easy question might very well be one of the first to be included in a problem-solving section to determine whether you are able to do basic multiplication. Other arithmetic manipulation questions might be more difficult:

Question 2-2

$(2,502)^2 - 2,500 \times 2,502 =$

(A) 2 (B) 4 (C) 2,500 (D) 5,000 (E) 5,004

This problem is more difficult than the preceding one; yet, it too can be solved by a basic calculation. It is unlikely that an arithmetic question of this difficulty would be included to test something so basic as the ability to multiply. Rather, it might be included to test whether you recognize an alternative way of performing the calculation. Instead of doing the operation as indicated, it is easier to arrive at the correct solution by seeing that the expression given is equivalent to

$$(2,502 \times 2,502) - (2,500 \times 2,502) =$$

and that 2,502 is common to both pairs of terms, so we can rewrite the expression as

$$2,502 \times (2,502 - 2,500) =$$

which is

$$2,502 \times 2$$

and that is 5,004. So the correct answer is (E).

Similar questions might be invented to test your ability to perform the basic manipulations of algebra:

Question 2-3

If $x + 2 = 5$, then $7(x - 3) =$

(A) −42 (B) −7 (C) 0 (D) 7 (E) 42

This is a fairly simple question. We should simply solve for x:

$$x + 2 = 5$$
$$x = 3$$

Substituting for x in the expression 7(x − 3), we have

$$7(3 − 3) = 7(0) = 0$$

So the correct answer is (C).

Of course, questions testing ability to do basic algebra can be more difficult:

Question 2-4

If $\dfrac{(x + y)^2}{x^2 - y^2} = 9$, then $\dfrac{x + y}{x - y} =$

(A) $\dfrac{1}{9}$ (B) $\dfrac{1}{3}$ (C) 1 (D) 3 (E) 9

The solution to this question is a bit more subtle than that of the preceding question. Here we may factor the expression $x^2 - y^2$:

$$\dfrac{(x + y)^2}{x^2 - y^2} = \dfrac{(x + y)(x + y)}{(x + y)(x - y)} = \dfrac{(x + y)}{(x - y)}$$

and that means that $\dfrac{x + y}{x - y}$ must be equal to 9, and the correct answer is (E).

Practical Word Problems

As the name implies, a practical word problem is designed to test your ability to apply quantitative tools in practical situations. On the GMAT, this may mean computing unit cost or profit, but the category is by no means so narrowly defined. Practical word problems often treat matters such as ratios, percentages, or distance. In any event, practical word problems that do use some common business situation as the focus for the question can be solved using common knowledge and ordinary mathematical procedures. No knowledge of specialized business procedures is required for the exam, as the following problem illustrates:

Question 2-5

For a certain year, a public utility reported earnings of $14.68 per share. The reported earnings per share for the fourth quarter were $4.42. If the number of shares listed did not change during the year, what were the average quarterly earnings for the first 3 quarters of the year?

(A) $3.42 (B) $3.67 (C) $5.62 (D) $6.84 (E) $10.26

The correct answer is (A). To determine the average earnings per share for the first 3 quarters, we first calculate the total earnings per share for the first 3 quarters:

$$\begin{array}{c} \text{Total per share} \\ \text{for year} \end{array} - \begin{array}{c} \text{Total per share} \\ \text{for 4th qtr.} \end{array} = \begin{array}{c} \text{Total per share} \\ \text{for first} \\ \text{three qtrs.} \end{array}$$

$$\$14.68 \ - \ \$4.42 \ = \ \$10.26$$

Then, we divide that by 3 to obtain the average quarterly earnings per share for each of the first 3 quarters:

$$\$10.26 \div 3 = \$3.42$$

Geometry Problems

Geometry problems involve the use of basic principles of geometry, usually to deduce some further conclusions from information given:

Question 2-6

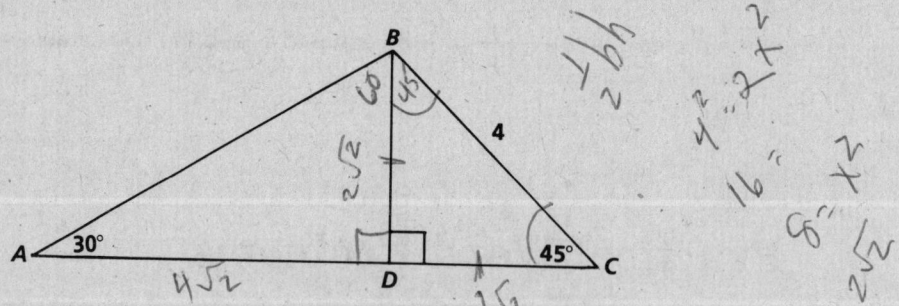

In the figure above, what is the area of triangle ABD?

(A) 2
(B) 4
(C) $4\sqrt{2}$
(D) $4\sqrt{3}$
(E) It cannot be determined from the information given.

The correct answer is (D). Since triangle BCD is a 45-45-90 triangle, sides BD and DC are equal. Using s as the length of BD and DC, we use the Pythagorean Theorem to find the length of BD:

$$\begin{array}{rcl} \text{Side Squared} + \text{Side Squared} & = & \text{Hypotenuse Squared} \\ s^2 \ + \ s^2 & = & 4^2 \\ 2s^2 & = & 16 \\ s^2 & = & 8 \\ s & = & 2\sqrt{2}. \end{array}$$

Then, triangle ABD is a 30-60-90 triangle, and in such a triangle the sides are in the ratio $\frac{h}{2} : \frac{h\sqrt{3}}{2} : h$. So:

$$AD = BD\sqrt{3}$$
$$AD = 2\sqrt{2}(\sqrt{3})$$
$$AD = 2\sqrt{6}.$$

Using the formula for the area of a triangle:

$$\text{Area} = \frac{1}{2}\,(\text{altitude} \times \text{base})$$

$$\text{Area} = \frac{1}{2}\,(2\sqrt{2})(2\sqrt{6}) = 2\sqrt{12} = 4\sqrt{3}.$$

PROBLEM-SOLVING ATTACK STRATEGY

The following flow-chart outlines the steps you need to take when you attack a problem-solving item:

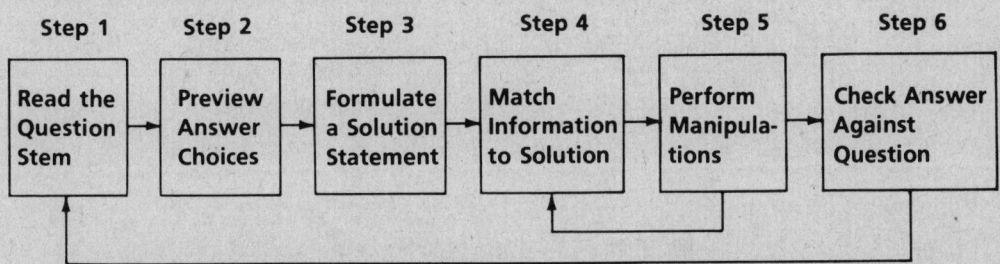

Step 1: Read the Question Stem

Obviously the first step is to read the question stem. And you must realize that careful reading is as important in this math section as it is in any verbal section.

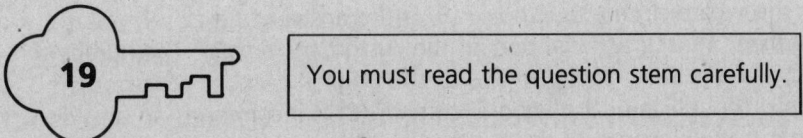

One common error made by test-takers in answering items in this section is to misread the question stem. Consequently, they seem to answer "correctly," but they answer the wrong question. Consider the following item:

Question 2-7

The people in a certain bank are either employees or customers, and the number of employees is 15 percent of the total number of people in the bank. After some of the customers leave, the total number of persons remaining in the bank is 50 percent of the original total. The number of customers who left is what fraction part of the original number of customers?

(A) $\frac{7}{20}$ (B) $\frac{7}{17}$ (C) $\frac{1}{2}$ (D) $\frac{10}{17}$ (E) $\frac{17}{20}$

The correct answer is (D), and one way of arriving at that conclusion is as follows.

Let N be the total number of people originally in the bank. The bank's employees accounted for 15 percent of that number, or $.15N$, which means that the customers accounted for $.85N$. Then, customers leave so that the number of people remaining in the bank is only 50 percent of the original total, that is, only $.50N$ people remain. The number of employees, however, has not changed, so we can calculate the fractional part of customers who now remain in the bank:

$$\text{New Total} - \text{Employees} = \text{Remaining Customers}$$
$$.50N - .15N = .35N.$$

But the question stem asks "The number of customers who left is what fractional part of the original number of customers?" So we must determine what fractional part of the customers left the bank:

$$\text{Original Number of Customers} - \text{Number of Customers Who Remain} = \text{Number of Customers Who Left}$$
$$.85N - .35N = .50N$$

We now set up a fraction:

$$\frac{\text{Number of Customers Who Left}}{\text{Original Number of Customers}}$$

$$\frac{.50N}{.85N} = \frac{10}{17}$$

The correct answer is (D).

Now consider the incorrect choices. Choice (B) is the answer to a closely related but different question: What fractional part of the customers *remain*? The number of customers remaining is $.35N$, so $\frac{.35N}{.85N} = \frac{7}{17}$ of the original number of customers are still in the bank. Though the calculation is correct, (B) is incorrect as an answer choice because it is not a response to the question asked.

Choice (E) can be analyzed in similar fashion. Initially, customers accounted for .85 of the total number of people in the bank, and $\frac{85}{100} = \frac{7}{20}$—again a correct calculation, but not responsive to the question asked. As for choice (A), the number of customers remaining in the bank is .35N, or $\frac{.35N}{1.00N} = \frac{7}{20}$. So the customers who remain constitute $\frac{7}{20}$ of the total number of people who were originally in the bank. So (A) is the correct answer to the question "The number of customers who remain constitute what fractional part of the original number of people in the bank?"

Finally, (C) may or may not represent a misreading of the question stem. A candidate could pick (C) by reasoning that one half of something remains so that half must be gone—forgetting that the employees must also be taken into account. Of course, not all errors made in handling problem-solving items are errors in reading. Many are errors in reasoning, but simple errors in reading are particularly annoying. A closely related error is answering in the wrong units.

Pay careful attention to the units in which the answer is to be expressed.

The danger of such a mistake can be minimized by making a little note in the margin of the test booklet to serve as a reminder of the units to be used in the final solution. Consider the following example:

Question 2-8

A certain machine produces 26 paper clips every 10 seconds. If the machine operates without interruption, how many paper clips will it produce in an hour?

(A) 156 (B) 936 (C) 3,600 (D) 5,616 (E) 9,360

The stem gives the rate of operation in clips per *second*, but your answer choice must be the number of clips produced in an *hour*. To remind yourself of the conversion that is required, you should make a note in the margin: clips/hour.

The correct answer to the question is (E). To solve the problem, first convert clips/second to clips/minute and then to clips/hour. This can be done by setting up a direct proportion:

$$\frac{26 \text{ clips}}{10 \text{ secs.}} = \frac{x \text{ clips}}{60 \text{ secs.}}$$

and solving for x:

$$\frac{(26)(60)}{10} = x$$

so

$$x = 156$$

This, however, is the number of clips produced in a *minute*—so (A) is not the correct answer. To find the number of clips produced in an hour, set up another direct proportion:

$$\frac{156 \text{ clips}}{1 \text{ minute}} = \frac{x \text{ clips}}{60 \text{ minutes}}$$

and solve for x

$$(156)(60) = x$$
$$x = 9{,}360$$

This number, 9,360, does represent the number of clips produced in an *hour*, and the correct answer is (E).

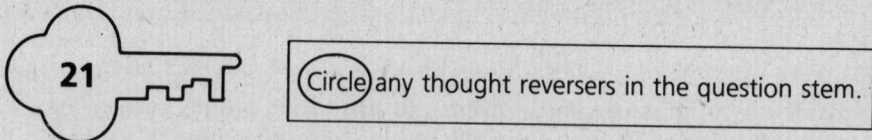

A thought reverser is any word such as "not," "but," or "except":

Question 2-9

A survey of 50 persons revealed that 36 of those surveyed had read a novel by author X and that 26 had read a novel by author Y. Which of the following could *not* be the total number of persons in the group that had read both a novel by X and a novel by Y?

(A) 10 (B) 12 (C) 16 (D) 32 (E) 40

The stem contains a thought reverser, *not*. We refer to such words as "thought reversers" because they reverse the ordinary meaning of the question. Usually a question in this section asks "What is . . . ?," and this question asks "What is *not* . . . ?" The correct answer is (A). Since there are only 50 people in the group, some of the people must have read novels by both authors. 36 plus 26 is 62, and that means *at least* 12 people must have read novels by both authors:

$$62 - 50 = 12$$

So the total number in the group who had read both authors could be 12, or 16, or 32, or even 40. The total number who had read both, however, could *not* be only 10. So (A) is the correct answer.

Step 2: Preview the Answer Choices

As a test taker, rather than a test writer, you see the importance of the correct choice, neglecting the importance of the incorrect choices. For the test writer, however, the incorrect choices are just as important, and they are developed according to strict guidelines.

Consider a sample array of answers in isolation—without a question stem:

xxxxxxxxxxxxxxxxxxxxxxxxxxxxxxxxxxxxxxxxxxxxxxxxxxxxxxxxxxxxxxxxxxxxx
xxxxxxxxxxxxxxxxxxxxxxxxxxxxxxxxxxxxxxxxxxxxxxxxxxxxxxxxxxxxxxxxxxxxx
xxxxxxxxxxxxxxxxxxxxxxxxxxxxxxxxxxxxxxxxxxxxxxxxxxxxxxxxxxxxxxxxxxxxx
xxxxxxxxxxxxxxxxxxxxxxxxxxxxxxxxxxx?

(A) $4,210   (B) $4,400   (C) $4,410   (D) $4,800   (E) $5,200

Even without the benefit of a question stem to guide us, we know that one, and only one of the choices can be correct. Each choice seems to be plausible. The choices are arranged in an order (from least to greatest). A preview can exploit these exam features in two important ways.

At first glance, each of the choices seems as likely to be correct as any of the others, but a closer look can eliminate some choices. Consider the following example:

Question 2-10

In 1980, Corporation X produced 40 percent of all passenger cars in Country P. If Corporation X produced 800,000 passenger cars, how many passenger cars were produced in Country P by all other producers combined?

(A) 320,000   (B) 480,000   (C) 1,200,000   (D) 1,600,000   (E) 2,000,000

Since Corporation X produced 800,000 cars and only 40 percent of all cars, could (A) or (B) be correct? No, the correct answer must be a number greater than 800,000. The correct answer is (C).

$$\frac{\text{Percent produced by } X}{\text{Number produced by } X} = \frac{\text{Percent produced by others}}{\text{Number produced by others}}$$

$$\frac{40\%}{800,000} = \frac{60\%}{T}$$

$$T = \frac{.60(800,000)}{.40} = 1,200,000$$

But the preview alone eliminates two of the five choices:

Eliminate any answer choice that cannot possibly be the answer to the question asked.

Sometimes it is even possible to reach a final solution to a question just at the stage of preview. To illustrate, we will add the stem to the "naked" answer choices above:

22 / 101 Tips for Scoring High on the GMAT

Question 2-11

$4,000 is deposited into a savings account that earns interest at 10 percent per year, compounded semiannually. How much money will there be in the account at the end of one year?

(A) $4,210   (B) $4,400   (C) $4,410   (D) $4,800   (E) $5,200

To solve the problem mathematically, we would have to compound the interest semiannually:

First six months
Principal × Rate × Time = Interest
$4,000 × .10 × .5 = $200.

We then add that $200 into the balance in the account and compute the interest for the second six months:

Principal × Rate × Time = Interest
$4,200 × .10 × .5 = $210.

Adding that to the account, the total at the end of one year will be $4,410.

It is possible, however, to solve the question by an intelligent preview. Without compounding the interest, the account would earn 10 percent of $4,000 in one year, or $400, leaving a total of $4,400 at the end of the year. Answer (B) is exactly $4,400. We know, however, that compound interest will be slightly more, so (B) must be wrong. Further, since the choices are arranged in order, (A), which is smaller than (B), must also be wrong. On the other side of (C), though interest compounded every six months will be slightly more than a simple 10 percent or $400, even the compound interest will not be $800—so (D), and with it (E), must also be wrong.

We extend the previous key to:

> If possible, use the distribution of choices to solve the problem at the preview step.

Consider the following example:

Question 2-12

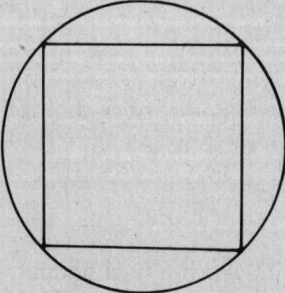

In the figure at the bottom of page 22, a square is inscribed in a circle. What is the ratio $\frac{\text{Area of Circle}}{\text{Area of Square}}$?

(A) π (B) 2 (C) $\frac{\pi}{2}$ (D) 1 (E) $\frac{2}{3\pi}$

At first glance, all of the choices may seem to be plausible, but study them closer. If the area of the circle were equal to the area of the square, then the ratio between them would be 1, and (D) would be correct. Obviously they are not equal, so (D), and along with it (E), must be incorrect. Further, it is equally clear that the circle is not twice as large as the square, so the ratio cannot be as large as 2:1, and both (B) and (A) are eliminated. So (C) is the correct answer. The choices are arranged in order, and one of them must be correct. If (B) is too large and (D) is too small, then (C) has to be the correct answer.

Step 3: Formulate a Solution Statement

Many questions are very complex, and require our third step. To formulate a solution statement locate the ultimate question to be answered, focus on that to the exclusion of all else, and consider what is required to answer the question:

Question 2-13

The populations of County X and County Y both grew by 8 percent from 1970 to 1980. If the population of County X grew by 80,000 and the population of County Y grew by 84,000, what was the difference between the population of County X in 1980 and that of County Y in 1980?

(A) 58,000   (B) 54,000   (C) 50,000   (D) 46,000   (E) 40,000

A preview does not allow us to find the correct answer to this question, so we must undertake a more involved solution.
We begin by focusing on the ultimate question to be answered:

The population of County X and County Y both grew by 8 percent from 1970 to 1980. If the population of County X grew by 80,000 and the population of County Y grew by 84,000, what was the difference between the population of County X in 1980 and that of County Y in 1980?

To avoid being distracted by all of the numbers at this step, we block out everything except the question to be answered: "...what was the difference between the population of County X in 1980 and that of County Y in 1980?"

If the question is a complex one, make a note of your solution statement in the margin of your test booklet.

The solution statement for the example under discussion might be rendered as:

County Y (1980) − County X (1980)

or even more concisely as:

Y('80) − X('80)

A solution statement is the point of your attack. Very few people (if any) are going to be able to solve this problem without some thought. Most of us will analyze this problem into a series of subproblems, working out a piece here and a piece there, and then putting those pieces together (Step 4). The solution statement will tell you what numbers you must ultimately have and will guide you in structuring the sub-tasks.

Step 4: Match Information to Solution

The fourth step of the flow-chart tells us to match information given in the question stem to the solution statement. In the preceding example, we need to find two numbers: County Y (1980) and County X (1980). The question stem states that County Y experienced an 8 percent increase in population between 1970 and 1980 and that this represented an increase of 84,000 people. In other words, 8 percent of the 1970 population, whatever that was, equaled 84,000. We translate this English statement into "equationese":

.08(1970 Population) = 84,000

and following the policy of using letters for unknowns, we use P_Y for 1970 population:

$.08(P_Y) = 84,000.$

At this juncture, you would probably proceed to Step 5 to perform manipulations and solve for P_Y. Before we do that, let us also set up a similar equation for County X:

8 percent of 1970 population County of X equaled 80,000.
$.08(P_X) = 80,000$

Step 5: Perform Manipulations

The fifth step is pure mechanics: solving for our unknowns:

$$.08(P_Y) = 84,000$$
$$P_Y = \frac{84,000}{.08} = 1,050,000$$
$$.08(P_X) = 80,000$$
$$P_X = \frac{80,000}{.08} = 1,000,000.$$

But these numbers, 1,050,000 and 1,000,000, represent the 1970 populations of Counties Y and X. For the solution statement we need the 1980 populations.

You will notice that there is an arrow in the flow-chart of the attack strategy that runs backward from Step 5 to Step 4. For a complicated problem it may be necessary to do one manipulation and pause to consider how that result can be used to get a further, needed result. In this case, we now know the 1970 populations of Counties X and Y, and we also know the 10-year increases in population for both. A repetition of Step 4 yields:

$$\text{1970 Population of } Y \text{ plus increase} = \text{1980 population of } Y$$
$$1,050,000 + 84,000 = 1,134,000$$
$$\text{1970 Population of } X \text{ plus increase} = \text{1980 population of } X$$
$$1,000,000 + 80,000 = 1,080,000.$$

Now we complete the solution statement and perform the final manipulation:

$$Y(1980) - X(1980) = \text{Difference}$$
$$1,134,000 - 1,080,000 = 54,000.$$

And the correct answer is (B).

Now let us move quickly to block a possible objection to this analysis. You may think the process too involved to be of any use on the actual exam, but remember that you can probably solve such a question more quickly than you can read about the solution. (Try writing an explanation for a simple calculation such as 128×12.) Our purpose in presenting such a detailed explanation was to provide a reconstruction of the solution process. Now you have a way of attacking such questions in an organized fashion, and as you practice with the method you will find that you get better at it.

Step 6: Check Answer Against Question

The final step in the attack strategy is to stop and ask yourself whether your result is a reasonable answer to the question asked. For the example we have been discussing, our result does seem reasonable and we know our answer is correct, but for other questions this final step may help you avoid a silly error.

Consider the following example:

Question 2-14

Machine X can fill a certain order in 6 hours, while Machine Y can fill the same order in 9 hours. What is the time, in hours, that it will take both machines working simultaneously to fill the order?

(A) 2.8   (B) 3.2   (C) 3.6   (D) 3.75   (E) 7.5

The final question to be answered is "How long will it take both machines working together?" For this we must find a way of combining the two rates. A natural error would be to average 6 and 9:

$$\frac{6+9}{2} = 7.5$$

and to conclude that both working together would require 7.5 hours to complete the work. On that basis, we would pick answer (E) (Error!). But is that a reasonable solution? Machine X alone can fill the order in only 6 hours, so is it reasonable to believe that both machines working together would take 7.5 hours, or 1.5 hours *longer* than Machine X alone? Clearly, this is not reasonable. The two machines working simultaneously will take less time than either working alone, and this commonsense observation saves us from error.

The correct answer is (C). When both machines are working simultaneously *add* their rates. Machine X does 1 order every 6 hours, so it operates at the rate $\frac{1 \text{ order}}{6 \text{ hours}}$. Machine Y does 1 order every 9 hours, so it operates at the rate of $\frac{1 \text{ order}}{9 \text{ hours}}$. Now we add:

$$\frac{1}{6} + \frac{1}{9} = \frac{15 \text{ orders}}{54 \text{ orders}}$$

This is the combined rate, but we want to know how long it would take to produce only 1 order. We set up a direct proportion:

$$\frac{15 \text{ orders}}{54 \text{ hours}} = \frac{1 \text{ order}}{x \text{ hours}}$$

and solve for x.

$$x = \frac{54}{15} = 3.6$$

This is answer (C). Is this a reasonable solution? If two Machine Xs were working, then it would take only half of 6 hours to fill the order, or 3 hours. If two Machine Ys were working, it would take half of 9 hours, or 4.5 hours, to fill the order. So both working together will fill the order in more than 3 hours but less than 4.5 hours, and (C) is a reasonable solution.

METHODS OF ATTACK FOR EACH PROBLEM TYPE

The flow-chart of a systematic attack is generally applicable to any item you might encounter in a problem-solving section; but there are different things you should look for in applying the strategy to different problem types. We will take each problem type in turn and discuss how the strategy outlined above might be applied to that type. Additionally, we offer suggestions as to what you might do if you find yourself unable to apply the strategy to some particularly recalcitrant test item.

Manipulation Problems

We've discussed two types of manipulation problems, arithmetic and algebra. Generally speaking, for an arithmetic manipulation problem, the solution statement will be nothing more than a restatement of the question posed. If you have a question such as

$$0.1 \times 0.002 =$$

then the ultimate question to be answered is "What is 0.1 times 0.002?" For such a question, the step of formulating a solution statement is pro forma. So too the fourth step of our strategy is taken en passant, for there is but one way to match the data to the solution statement: you have to do the multiplication. But when we reach the fifth step and perform manipulations, we encounter a complication. Compare the following two questions:

Question 2-15

0.25 × 0.004 =

(A) 0.0001 (B) 0.001 (C) 0.01 (D) 0.1 (E) 1.0

Question 2-16

Of the following, which best approximates $\frac{(0.8333)(0.3333)(0.2222)}{(0.6667)(0.1667)(0.1111)}$

(A) 4.00 (B) 4.25 (C) 4.60 (D) 5.00 (E) 5.45

Question 2-15 requires a fairly simple manipulation, but *Question 2-16* requires an almost unmanageable manipulation—unmanageable because you are not permitted to use a calculator on the exam!

The correct strategy for the first is to perform the indicated operation exactly as shown:

For an easy arithmetic question, do the indicated operations.

Multiplying .25 by .004 yields .001, so the correct answer is (B).

For *Question 2-16* we will need an alternative, for the calculation indicated is not manageable:

If an arithmetic question indicates unmanageable operations, look for an alternative such as canceling, factoring, or approximating.

Each of the decimal numbers in the second, more difficult problem is an example of a fraction:

$$0.8333 = \frac{5}{6} \quad 0.3333 = \frac{1}{3} \quad 0.2222 = \frac{2}{9}$$
$$0.6667 = \frac{2}{3} \quad 0.1667 = \frac{1}{6} \quad 0.1111 = \frac{1}{9}$$

If we substitute these fractions for the decimals in the original problem, we have a more manageable calculation:

$$\frac{(\frac{5}{6})(\frac{1}{3})(\frac{2}{9})}{(\frac{2}{3})(\frac{1}{6})(\frac{1}{9})}$$

but even these operations would be time consuming. We can, however, simplify things even further. Since to divide by a fraction is to invert the fraction and multiply, let us first rewrite the expression as follows:

$$\left(\frac{5}{6}\right)\left(\frac{1}{3}\right)\left(\frac{2}{9}\right)\left(\frac{3}{2}\right)\left(\frac{6}{1}\right)\left(\frac{9}{1}\right)$$

Now matters can be simplified considerably by canceling:

$$\left(\frac{5}{\cancel{6}}\right)\left(\frac{1}{\cancel{3}}\right)\left(\frac{\cancel{2}}{\cancel{9}}\right)\left(\frac{\cancel{3}}{\cancel{2}}\right)\left(\frac{\cancel{6}}{1}\right)\left(\frac{\cancel{9}}{1}\right) = 5$$

and the correct answer must be (D).

For an example of a manipulation question using factoring, see *Question 2-4*. The algebra manipulation problems receive similar treatment.

27   If the question contains a simple equation with one variable, solve for the unknown.

Question 2-17

If $2x - 6 = x + 3$, then $x =$

(A) -3 (B) -1 (C) 1 (D) 3 (E) 9

The question is fairly simple. The solution statement is "What is x?" and the only basis for an answer is the equation. So we solve for x:

$$2x - 6 = x + 3$$
$$x = 9$$

and the correct answer is (E). If you wish to check the reasonableness of this solution, you do so by substituting 9 for x in the equation:

$$2(9) - 6 = 9 + 3$$
$$18 - 6 = 9 + 3$$
$$12 = 12$$

which shows our solution to be correct.

A variation on this theme would be:

Question 2-18

If $x + y = 18$ and $x - y = 2$, then $x =$

(A) -2 (B) 0 (C) 2 (D) 8 (E) 10

Here we must solve for x. We solve for one variable in one equation:

$$y = 18 - x$$

and substitute this into the other equation:

$$x - (18 - x) = 2$$

and solve for x:

$$2x - 18 = 2$$
$$2x = 20$$
$$x = 10$$

and the correct answer is (E).

If a question contains two equations and two variables, treat the equations as simultaneous equations to find a solution for the unknown asked about.

Sometimes it will not be either possible or necessary to arrive at a numerical value for an unknown:

Question 2-19

If $7 - 2x = y + 2$, then $5 - 2x =$

(A) $\dfrac{y+1}{2}$ (B) $2y + 4$ (C) y (D) $y - 2$ (E) $y - 4$

Here it is not possible to arrive at numerical values for either x or y, but then that is not necessary. $5 - 2x$ differs from $7 - 2x$ by only 2. If we subtract 2 from $7 - 2x$, we get $5 - 2x$. This means that $5 - 2x = y + 2 - 2$, and that is just y. So the correct answer is (C).

We now have an additional strategy:

If it is impossible to fill out the needed solution with numbers, try rewriting the given algebraic information so that it matches the solution you need.

Consider the following two questions:

Question 2-20

If $\frac{p}{q} = 0.0742$, then $\frac{p}{2q} =$

(A) 0.0371
(B) 0.0740
(C) 0.0744
(D) 0.1484
(E) It cannot be determined from the information given.

Question 2-21

If $a + b = \frac{3}{5}$, and $a - b = \frac{5}{3}$, then $\frac{a+b}{a-b} =$

(A) 0   (B) $\frac{1}{3}$ (C) $\frac{9}{25}$ (D) 1   (E) $\frac{25}{9}$

In *Question 2-20*, it is impossible to solve for either p or q. So we ask, "What is the connection between $\frac{p}{q}$ and $\frac{p}{2q}$?" The only difference is the 2 in the denominator. This means that $\frac{p}{2q}$ is half of $\frac{p}{q}$. So if $\frac{p}{q}$ is 0.0742, then $\frac{p}{2q}$ is $\frac{1}{2}(0.0742)$ or 0.0371. So the correct answer is (A).

In *Question 2-21*, it would be possible to solve for both a and b because we have two equations. It is simpler, however, to see that values are given both for $a + b$ and for $a - b$. To find the value of $\frac{a+b}{a-b}$, we need only divide the value of $a + b$ by the value of $a - b$:

$$\frac{\frac{3}{5}}{\frac{5}{3}} = \frac{3}{5} \times \frac{3}{5} = \frac{9}{25}$$

So the correct answer is (C).

Now we consider how to apply our strategy to problems of a slightly different format:

Question 2-22

The difference between which of the following pairs of numbers is equal to 7 times their product?

(A) 1, 7   (B) 1, $\frac{7}{8}$ (C) 1, $\frac{6}{7}$ (D) 1, $\frac{1}{7}$ (E) 1, $\frac{1}{8}$

If you put your hand over the answer choices, the question makes no sense. The question is designed so that you must use information provided in the choices to arrive at your solution.

Here the correct choice is (E):

$$\begin{array}{cc} \text{Difference} & 7 \times \text{Product} \\ 1 - \frac{1}{8} & 7(1 \times \frac{1}{8}) \\ \frac{7}{8} & = \frac{7}{8} \end{array}$$

We generalize on this example to provide the key for all such questions:

For a question that asks for an answer choice meeting certain conditions, test each choice to find the one that satisfies the solution statement.

Consider:

Question 2-23

$7^3 \cdot 8 =$

(A) $10 \cdot 8$ (B) $21 \cdot 8$ (C) $56 \cdot 3$ (D) $49 \cdot 56$ (E) $49 \cdot 64$

The correct answer to this question must be (D).

$$7^3 \cdot 8 = 7 \cdot 7 \cdot 7 \cdot 8 = 49 \cdot 56$$

The only way to find this is by testing each choice. (A) cannot be correct since 7^3 times 8 is larger than 80. We can eliminate (B) on the same ground. (C) too can be eliminated since the expression in the stem is equal to 56 times 49, not 56 times 3. Finally, (E) can be eliminated, for the expression in the stem is equal to 49 times 56, not 49 times 64.

There is a variation on this theme we should consider. Sometimes a question will ask that you pick the largest or smallest of a group of answer choices.

When trying to determine which answer choice is the largest or smallest, use a benchmark.

Consider the following example:

Question 2-24

Which of the following is the largest?

(A) $\frac{1}{2} + \frac{1}{3}$ (B) $(\frac{1}{2} + \frac{1}{3})^2$ (C) $(\frac{1}{2} + \frac{1}{3})^3$ (D) $(\frac{1}{2})^2 + (\frac{1}{3})^2$ (E) $(\frac{1}{2})^3 + (\frac{1}{3})^3$

We proceed in the following way.

First, we compare (A) with (B). We note that $\frac{1}{2} + \frac{1}{3}$ is less than 1. (B) must be smaller than (A), since a fraction raised to a power is smaller than the original fraction itself. (B) is eliminated, and (A) becomes the benchmark or standard by which we measure the other choices. When we compare (C) with (A), we eliminate (C) on the same ground that we eliminated (B): a fraction raised to a power is less than the original fraction. Next we compare (D) with (A). (D) is similar to (A) in that the fractions $\frac{1}{2}$ and $\frac{1}{3}$ appear in both, but in (D) the fractions are squared. Since $(\frac{1}{2})^2$ is smaller than $\frac{1}{2}$ and $(\frac{1}{3})^2$ is smaller than $\frac{1}{3}$, (D) is smaller than (A) and is thereby eliminated. Finally, we eliminate (E) on the same ground. By the process of comparison and elimination, (A) must be the largest. Therefore, the correct answer is (A).

Practical Word Problems

In our initial discussion of the flow-chart, we applied the step-by-step attack strategy in some detail to a practical word problem (*Question 2-13*). Sometimes the data on the GMAT are presented graphically. The graphs or charts used on the test are fairly simple, and you need no special instruction to read them. The only real difference between a practical word problem based on a graph and an ordinary practical word problem is that the data for the graph problem are presented in picture form:

Questions 2-25 and 2-26 refer to the following graphs:

Outlays By Corporation X in Year Y

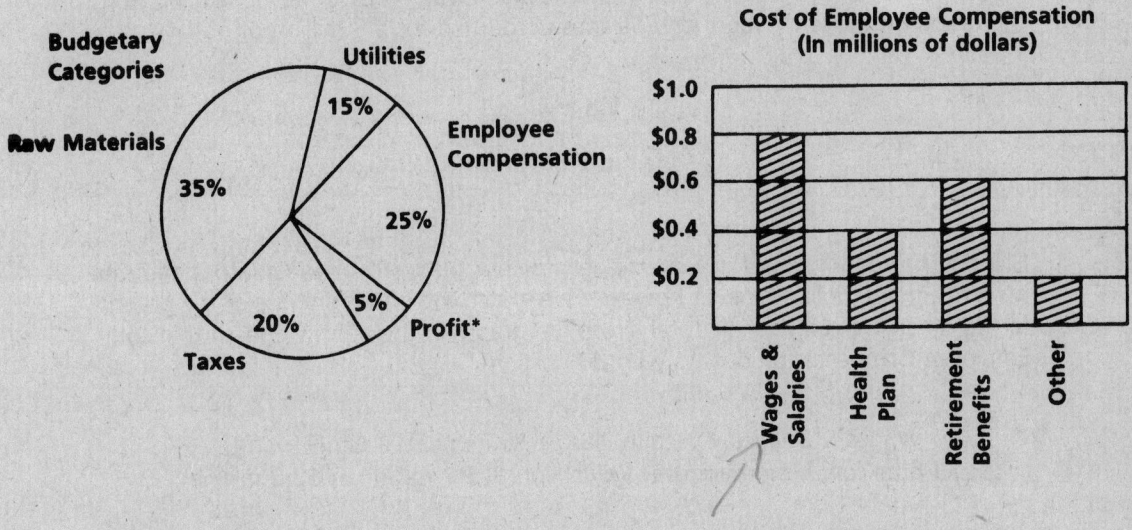

Budgetary Categories (pie chart):
- Raw Materials 35%
- Utilities 15%
- Employee Compensation 25%
- Profit* 5%
- Taxes 20%

Cost of Employee Compensation (In millions of dollars):
- Wages & Salaries: $0.8
- Health Plan: $0.4
- Retirement Benefits: $0.6
- Other: $0.2

Question 2-25

For year Y, Wages and Salaries accounted for what percent of total outlays by Corporation X?

(A) 8%   (B) 10%   (C) 12½%   (D) 25%   (E) 80%

Question 2-26

If the cost of steel was equal to the amount of profit distributed, then the outlay for steel was what fraction of the total outlay for raw materials?

(A) $\frac{1}{30}$ (B) $\frac{1}{20}$ (C) $\frac{1}{7}$ (D) $\frac{7}{20}$ (E) $\frac{2}{5}$

When the information is presented in graphic form, your reading must also include the graphs. For *Questions 2-25* and *2-26* we have two related graphs. The graph on the left is a pie graph that shows what *percent* of the outlays went to which category. The pie graph, by itself, does not give dollar values for those outlays, only fractions of an unknown total. The graph on the right uses bars to show the dollar value of outlays for Employee Compensation in "millions of dollars" as units; for example, Wages and Salaries total $.8 million or $800,000.

A preview of *Question 2-25* should allow you to exclude two choices from consideration. The category Employee Compensation accounted for 25 percent of all outlays. Since Wages and Salaries is only a subpart of that category, Wages and Salaries must have accounted for less than 25 percent of all outlays. Thus, we eliminate (D) and (E). Next we isolate the ultimate question: Wages and Salaries accounted for what percent of total outlays? And we make a note of our solution statement:

$$\frac{\text{Wages \& Salaries}}{\text{Total Outlays}}$$

or if you prefer

$$\frac{W \& S}{T}$$

Now we go to the data presented in the graphs and try to match the data to the solution statement. The numerator of the fraction is fairly easy to fill in. Reading from the graph on the left, Wages and Salaries accounted for $.8 million of outlays:

$$\frac{\$.8 \text{ million}}{T}$$

Filling in the denominator is a bit trickier, for our pie chart gives its information in percents, not in dollar value. If, however, we match the data from one of the graphs to the other, we can find the total. From the graph on the right, we learn that total Employee Compensation outlays were $2 million:

Wages & Salaries + Health Plan + Retirement + Other = Total
$.8 million + $.4 million + $.6 million + $.2 million = $2.0 million

And this $2.0 million is 25 percent of all outlays, according to the pie chart. So

$$\begin{aligned} 25\% \text{ of Total Outlays} &= 2 \text{ million} \\ .25\,(T) &= 2 \text{ million} \\ T &= 8 \text{ million} \end{aligned}$$

We enter this in our solution statement:

$$\frac{\$.8 \text{ million}}{\$8.0 \text{ million}} = 10\%$$

And (B) is the correct answer.

Is this a reasonable answer? Yes, since Wages and Salaries account for a substantial proportion, though less than half the total Cost of Employees, and this category in turn accounted for ½ of all outlays. So our correct choice should be slightly less than half of 50 percent.

Now we turn to *Question 2-26*. A preview of this item does not provide any startling or powerful insights, so we formulate a solution statement:

$$\frac{\text{Cost of Steel}}{\text{Cost of Raw Materials}}$$

or if you prefer:

$$\frac{\text{Steel}}{\text{Raw}}$$

It would be possible to find the numbers for our solution by calculating the total outlays as we did in the previous question, or even using that information here. It is also possible to answer this question without using dollar values. It is a characteristic of a pie graph that all of the percentages shown are taken from the same total, that is, they are all part of the same pie. So we use the value .35T, or 35 percent of total pie, for Cost of Raw Materials.

$$\frac{\text{Steel}}{.35T}$$

Then we are instructed to assume that the cost of steel was equal to Profit, and that would be 5 percent of T:

$$\frac{.05T}{.35T}$$

Notice that the Ts cancel, which is to say that whatever the actual dollar value of the "pie," $\frac{5}{35}$ or $\frac{1}{7}$ is the fraction of the total allocated to steel outlays. So (C) is our answer.

Is (C) a reasonable response? Yes, and one way of demonstrating this is to look at the portion of the pie for Profit, which we are told equals steel, and the portion for all Raw Materials. The one sector appears to be between ⅕ and 1/10 the size of the other.

For some practical word problems there is an alternative strategy:

32 — Work backwards from the answer choices to the solution statement, starting with the middle value.

Consider the following example:

Question 2-27

A merchant gives her customers a 20 percent discount on the usual selling price of an item. If she is still able to realize a net profit of 25 percent on the $16.00 cost of the item, what is the usual selling price of the item?

(A) $20.00   (B) $20.60   (C) $24.00   (D) $25.00   (E) $26.67

We know that one of the five choices must be correct, so all we have to do is test each choice to find which is the usual selling price. We begin with (C).

Assuming for the purpose of analysis that the usual selling price is $24.00:

$$\text{Usual Selling Price} - .20(\text{Usual Selling Price}) = \text{Actual Selling Price}$$
$$24.00 - .20(24.00) = \$19.20$$

Then,

$$\text{Actual Selling Price} - \text{Cost} = \text{Profit}$$
$$\$19.20 - \$16.00 = \$3.20$$

And finally,

$$\frac{\$3.20}{\$16.00} \neq 25\%$$

This proves that (C) is not the correct choice, and now we test either (B) or (D). Since an assumed Usual Selling Price of $25.00 generated a profit of approximately $\frac{3}{16}$, which is less than $\frac{1}{5}$ and so less than 25 percent, we should try the next higher number as the Usual Selling Price. So we test (D):

$$\$25.00 - .20(\$25.00) = \$20.00$$

and

$$\$20.00 - \$16.00 = \$4.00$$

Finally,

$$\frac{\$4.00}{\$16.00} = 25\%$$

Which proves (D) is the correct answer.

Even if the choices had been arranged differently; for example,

(A) $10.00   (B) $20.00   (C) $20.60   (D) $24.00   (E) $25.00

only two calculations would have been needed. Had the choices been arranged as shown, we would have tested (C) and then (D). When $24.00 proved incorrect, we would immediately conclude that the one remaining choice, (E) $25.00, had to be the right one. To reinforce the point, let us study another example:

Question 2-28

A group of investors purchased an apartment building that returned total net income over a 10-year period equal to the $138,000 original investment. If expenses consumed 25 percent of the annual gross income from the building, what was the average annual gross income from the building over the 10-year period?

(A) $3,450   (B) $13,800   (C) $17,250   (D) $18,400   (E) $34,500

You would begin working backward with the middle value, (C). On the assumption that annual gross income was $17,250, average net income would have been:

$$\text{Gross} - \text{Expenses} = \text{Net}$$
$$\$17,250 - .25(\$17,250) = \$12,937.50$$

but $12,937.50 × 10 is only $129,375—not $138,000. So (C) is incorrect, and since we came out with less income than was stipulated by the stem, we should try the next larger number:

$$\text{Gross} - \text{Expenses} = \text{Net}$$
$$\$18,400 - .25(\$18,400) = \$13,800$$

And $13,800 × 10 is $138,000. So the average annual gross income of $18,400 matches the information in the stem, and our correct answer is (D).

We will provide yet another example to be attacked in the same way:

Question 2-29

A hotel has 600 rooms that rent for $36, $54, or $72 a night. ⅓ of the rooms rent for $54 a night. When the hotel is completely booked, gross receipts for the night are $30,600. How many of the rooms rent for $36 a night?

(A) 100   (B) 150   (C) 160   (D) 200   (E) 250

We begin by noting that if ⅓ of the 600 rooms, or 200 rooms, rent for $54 a night, those rooms generate income of $10,800. This means that the remaining rooms, priced at $36 a night or $72 a night, must account for the rest of the money or $19,800. How many $36-a-night rooms does the hotel have?

We first test (C), 160. If the hotel has 160 rooms that rent for $36 a night, then it has 240 rooms renting for $72 a night.

$$
\begin{array}{rl}
160 @ \$36 = & \$\ 5,760 \\
240 @ \$72 = & \underline{\$17,280} \\
\text{Total} & \$23,040
\end{array}
$$

But $23,040 \neq $19,800, and (C) cannot be correct. If we get too much money by assuming 160 of the cheapest rooms and 240 of the most expensive rooms, we should alter our assumption to reduce the number of expensive rooms, and increase the number of cheap rooms, thereby lowering the income. So our next test would be (D):

$$
\begin{array}{rl}
200 @ \$36 = & \$ 7,200 \\
200 @ \$72 = & \$14,400 \\
\text{Total} & \$21,600
\end{array}
$$

But $21,600 \neq $19,800, which proves, by elimination, that (E) is correct. There is no need to test (E), but to reassure you that (E) is truly the correct choice:

$$
\begin{array}{rl}
250 @ \$36 = & \$ 9,000 \\
150 @ \$72 = & \$10,800 \\
\text{Total} & \$19,800
\end{array}
$$

And that is the number we were trying to match.

Some practical word problems supply data in algebraic form, and then answer choices are algebraic formulas:

Question 2-30

At a certain factory, each of m machines produces 3 clothespins every s seconds. If all machines work together without interruption, how many *minutes* will it take to produce 9,000 clothespins?

(A) $\dfrac{180s}{m}$ (B) $\dfrac{50s}{m}$ (C) $50ms$ (D) $\dfrac{ms}{50}$ (E) $\dfrac{300m}{s}$

To find how long, in minutes, the factory will need to produce 9,000 clothespins, we must divide the 9,000 clothespins by the number of clothespins produced in a minute:

$$\frac{9{,}000 \text{ clothespins}}{\text{clothespins per minute}}$$

But the question does not directly tell us how many clothespins the factory produces in a minute.

Each machine produces 3 clothespins every s seconds. Since there are 60 seconds in a minute, each machine in a minute produces:

$$\frac{3}{s} \text{ times } 60 = \frac{180}{s} \text{ clothespins}$$

And there are m such machines, so the total output will be m times that:

$$m \text{ times } \frac{180}{s} = \frac{180m}{s}$$

So the factory produces $\frac{180m}{s}$ clothespins per minute, and we substitute this expression into the denominator of our solution statement:

$$\frac{9{,}000}{\frac{180m}{s}} = 9{,}000 \times \frac{s}{180m} = \frac{50s}{m}.$$

So the correct answer is (B).

Many test takers will find a question such as *Question 2-30* vexing because the information is presented algebraically rather than with actual numbers. So, we suggest:

33 — If the choices are algebraic expressions using unknowns from the question stem, substitute values to find the correct choice.

Since the information is given algebraically, the letter variables in the problem could stand for almost any number (avoiding dividing by zero and so on). So you can simply pick some values.

For *Question 2-30* assume that s is 3, which is to say that each machine produces 3 clothespins every 3 seconds or 1 clothespin per second. On that assumption, such a machine produces 60 clothespins in a minute. How many machines are there? Assume a nice easy number such as 2. In that case, the factory would produce 120 clothespins per minute. To produce 9,000 clothespins at that rate would take:

$$\frac{9{,}000}{120} = 75$$

Now look at the answer choices. Assuming that $s = 3$ and $m = 2$, it takes the factory 75 minutes to produce 9,000 clothespins. Substituting 3 for s and 2 for m into the formulas in the choices, which formula generates the number 75?

Choice (A): $\dfrac{180(3)}{2} = 270 \neq 75$

Choice (B): $\dfrac{50(3)}{2} = 75$ (Correct answer)

Choice (C): $50(2)(3) = 300 \neq 75$

Choice (D): $\dfrac{(2)(3)}{50} = \dfrac{6}{50} \neq 75$

Choice (E): $\dfrac{300(2)}{3} = 200 \neq 75$

So (B) is the correct choice.

To prove the value of the technique, we will solve the following example using only this new strategy:

Question 2-31

A train is traveling at an average speed of 120 kilometers per hour. On the average, how many seconds are needed for the train to travel K kilometers?

(A) $\dfrac{K}{120}$ (B) $\dfrac{K}{30}$ (C) 2K   (D) 30K   (E) 432,000K

First pick a value for K, K = 120.

Since the train travels, on this assumption, 120 kilometers every hour, it travels 120 kilometers every 3,600 seconds (60 seconds × 60 minutes = 3,600 seconds in an hour). Using K = 120, the correct answer choice will generate the number 3,600.

Choice (A): $\dfrac{120}{120}$ = 1 ≠ 3,600

Choice (B): $\dfrac{120}{30}$ = 4 ≠ 3,600

Choice (C):   2(120)   = 240 ≠ 3,600

Choice (D):   30(120)   = 3,600 (Correct answer)

Choice (E):   432,000(3,600) ≠ 3,600

Substitution shows that (D) is the correct formula.

You may wonder why we picked the numbers that we did and how you will know which numbers might be useful in a different question. With certain exceptions such as dividing by zero, the formula will hold good for any substitution instances. We selected numbers which were convenient. Convenient numbers are ones that are small; for example, 1 or 2, or ones that match up with numbers in the problem. In attacking Question 2-30, we picked the value 3 for s because the information stated that each machine produced 3 clothespins per s seconds, and that gave us a nice, convenient number of 1 clothespin per second. Or again, in Question 2-31 we used 120 for K, because the train was traveling at 120 kilometers per hour.

To get practice in selecting convenient numbers, do the following problem using the alternative attack strategy.

Question 2-32

A copy center has an ordinary copier and a high-speed copier. The high-speed copier makes copies 11 times as fast as the ordinary copier. If the high-speed copier makes n copies per second, how many copies can both machines working simultaneously produce in 4 minutes?

(A) $\dfrac{n+1}{11}$ (B) $\dfrac{12n}{11}$ (C) $\dfrac{48n}{11}$ (D) 480n   (E) $\dfrac{2,880n}{11}$

To determine how many copies the two machines will produce together in 4 minutes, you can assume a rate for one or the other copier. Then you will compute the rate of the second copier, add the two rates, and multiply that by the number of seconds in 4 minutes. We would have assigned n the value of 11. We know that we have to express the rate of the ordinary copier in terms of the rate of the faster copier; for example, if the faster copier produces 6 copies per second, then the slower copier produces $\frac{6}{11}$ copies per second. So we pick 11 for n, since $\frac{11}{11}$ is 1, a convenient number.

On the assumption that $n = 11$, the faster copier produces 11 copies per second, and the ordinary copier produces 1 copy per second. Together, then, they would produce 12 copies per second. 12 copies per second times 60 seconds times 4 minutes equals 2,880 copies in 4 minutes. Substituting 11 for n in the choices:

Choice (A): $\dfrac{11 + 1}{11} = \dfrac{12}{11} \neq 2{,}880$

Choice (B): $\dfrac{12(11)}{11} = 12 \neq 2{,}880$

Choice (C): $\dfrac{48(11)}{11} = 48 \neq 2{,}880$

Choice (D): $480(11) = 5{,}280 \neq 2{,}880$

Choice (E): $\dfrac{2{,}880(11)}{11} = 2{,}880$ (Correct answer)

There is one complication that we should mention. One of the most convenient values to work with is 1. But you may find with 1 that more than one formula seems to produce a correct result:

Question 2-33

A clock gains m minutes every h hours. If the clock shows the correct time at noon on Monday, what time will it show at noon on Wednesday of the same week?

(A) $\dfrac{48m}{h}$ after noon

(B) $\dfrac{48h}{m}$ after noon

(C) $\dfrac{2880h}{m}$ after noon

(D) $48mh$ after noon

(E) $\dfrac{48m}{h}$ before noon

Assume that the clock gains 1 minute every hour. On that assumption, 2 days later the clock should be 48 minutes fast. So on Wednesday, when the true time is noon, the clock will show a time 48 minutes ahead of that, or 48 minutes after noon. So on the assumption that $m = 1$ and $h = 1$, the correct formula should generate the number 48. Substituting 1 for m and 1 for h into the answer choices, (A), (B), (D), and (E) all generate the value 48. We eliminate (C) because it does not, and we can also eliminate (E) since it asserts that the clock is running slow, not fast. We are still left with (A), (B), and (D). What happened?

Since we picked 1 to substitute, we coincidentally found more than one formula. This is because $1 = \frac{1}{1} = 1 \times 1$, so (A), (B), and (D) look exactly alike using only 1 as a substitution. Therefore, we should pick another set of numbers. Let us assume that the clock gains 1 minute every half hour. On that assumption, after 48 hours the clock should be $1 \times 48 \times 2 = 96$ minutes fast. Substituting 1 for m and $\frac{1}{2}$ for h, only (A) generates the number 96. So (A) must be the correct answer.

When plugging in numerical values, you should select numbers that are easy to work with. Of course, you run a risk of finding more than one seemingly correct choice, but in that event, you just select another set of numbers until you eliminate all but one choice. That will be the correct answer.

There is yet another variation on this theme in which the question stem does not even refer by letter to the quantities being discussed:

Question 2-34

If the value of a motor vehicle decreases by 20 percent while the tax rate on motor vehicles increases by 20 percent, what is the effect on the taxes?

(A) Taxes increase by 16 percent
(B) Taxes increase by 4 percent
(C) There is no change in taxes
(D) Taxes decrease by 4 percent
(E) Taxes decrease by 16 percent

The "orthodox" method of solving the question is to assign letters for the quantities that are not defined. Let V stand for the value of the motor vehicle and T stand for the tax rate. Initially, the taxes would be TV. Then increase the tax rate by 20 percent, from T to $1.2T$; and decrease the value of the vehicle from V to $.8V$. Then the taxes will be $.8V$ times $1.2T = .96TV$. So there was a drop of $.04TV$ or 4 percent.

If the "orthodox" approach is not comfortable for you, use the method of substituting values:

34 — For questions with undefined quantities, assume arbitrary values.

Since in *Question 2-34*, neither the value of the motor vehicle nor the tax rate is defined, either by number or by letter, we are free to assume values. Let us assume that the original value of the motor vehicle is $1,000 (a convenient number) and that the tax rate was 10 percent (again, a convenient assumption). Initially, the taxes would have been $1,000(.10) = $100. Then, we reduce the value of the motor vehicle by 20 percent:

$$\$1{,}000 - .20(\$1{,}000) = \$800$$

We increase the tax rate by 20 percent:

$$10\% + .20(10\%) = 12\%$$

The new taxes will be:

$$\$800 \times .12 = \$96$$

So the taxes drop from $100 to $96, a percentage drop of

$$\frac{100 - 96}{100} = .04 = 4\%$$

Now consider a more difficult question:

Question 2-35

In a certain business enterprise John contributed $\frac{4}{5}$ as much capital as Mary contributed, and Mary contributed $\frac{1}{3}$ as much capital as Susan contributed. If these three people contributed all of the capital, then what fraction of the capital did Mary contribute?

(A) $\frac{1}{24}$ (B) $\frac{1}{6}$ (C) $\frac{5}{24}$ (D) $\frac{12}{31}$ (E) $\frac{15}{24}$

Since the question stem does not stipulate any particular dollar contribution, we can assume any numbers we wish. Of course, we would like to use numbers that can be conveniently manipulated. Looking at the fractions in the question stem, $\frac{4}{5}$ and $\frac{1}{3}$, we see that a common multiple of 5 and 3 would be a good number. So we assume that the largest investor, Susan, contributed $15. If Susan contributed $15, then Mary contributed $\frac{1}{3}(\$15) = \$5$. And John contributed $\frac{4}{5}(\$5) = \$4$. The total capitalization was $15 + $5 + $4 = $24, of which Mary contributed $5. So Mary's share was $\frac{5}{24}$, and (C) is the correct answer.

With practice you will acquire a sense of which numbers would be convenient to work with, but even inconvenient numbers will generate the correct solution. For example, suppose we had assumed that John contributed $5. This would mean that Mary contributed $\frac{5}{4}$ as much, or $\$\frac{25}{4}$, and Susan contributed 3 times that or $\$\frac{75}{4}$. The total investment, on that assumption, would be $\frac{120}{4}$, of which $\frac{25}{4}$ was Mary's contribution. That is a fraction of $\frac{25/4}{120/4} = \frac{25}{120} = \frac{5}{24}$.

We do not mean to imply that these alternative attack strategies can be applied mechanically, without thought; nor that they are generally applicable to every problem on the test. With practice, you will learn which problems are susceptible to which strategies; and, given the scoring of the exam, even two or three more questions can make an important difference in your final score. This brings us to our last suggestion:

35 Use common sense to eliminate implausible answers.

Question 2-36

A certain dairy packing plant has two machines, P and Q, that process milk at constant rates of 30 gallons per minute and 45 gallons per minute, respectively. A day's run of milk can be processed by machine P operating alone in 6 hours, by machine Q operating alone in 4 hours, or by both machines operating simultaneously in 2.4 hours. If a day's run of milk is processed, using machine Q alone for half the time and both machines together for half the time, how many hours does it take to complete the run?

(A) 1.5   (B) 3.0   (C) 3.75   (D) 4.2   (E) 5.0

Given that Q alone could do the job in 4 hours and that P and Q together would need 2.4 hours, the running time asked for must be shorter than 4 hours yet longer than 2.4 hours. This eliminates (A), (D), and (E) as choices, and we are still not finished. As a matter of common sense, since the running time is divided evenly between machine Q alone and P and Q together, the time should be somewhere in between 2.4 and 4, near the middle. It will not be exactly 3.2 since P and Q, during their half of the operating time, will do more than half the job, while Q alone, during its half of the operating time will do less than half the job. Even so, the number must be close to 3.2. It cannot take as long as 3.75 hours, and (C) cannot be correct. In fact, our reasoning shows that (B) must be correct since the running time will be slightly less than 3.2 hours.

Geometry Problems

Our attack strategy is also applicable to geometry problems which are in many respects similar to practical word problems. They are challenging either because the solution statement is not obvious or because it is not immediately clear how to match the data to the solution statement.

We have already seen the importance of the preview in the context of geometry problems (Question 2-12), so there is no need to cover that ground again. We will proceed directly to discuss two different types of geometry problems. Or rather we should say, we will discuss geometry problems in which the point of emphasis is on matching the data to the solution and others in which the point of emphasis is on formulating the solution statement.

We begin by discussing questions in which the main problem is matching the data against a fairly obvious solution statement:

Question 2-37

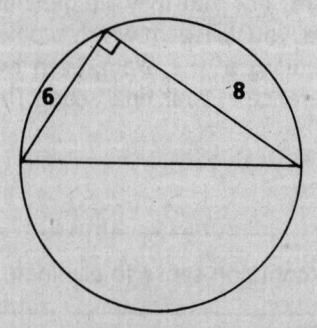

Problem Solving / 45

What is the circumference of the circle in the figure at the bottom of page 44?

(A) 4.5π (B) 5π (C) 10π (D) 25π (E) 100π

The solution statement for this problem is well known:

$$\text{Circumference} = 2\pi r$$

What makes the question interesting is that we must match the data against the solution statement. The key to this question is that the hypotenuse of the right triangle is also the diameter of the circle. The hypotenuse will be:

$$6^2 + 8^2 = h^2$$
$$h^2 = 100$$
$$h = 10$$

(or you might have observed that 6:8:10 as 3:4:5). If the hypotenuse is equal to the diameter of the circle, then the diameter of the circle is 10, and the radius of the circle is 5. Thus, the circumference is:

$$\text{Circumference} = 2\pi r$$
$$C = 10\pi$$

The correct answer is (C).
Many exam problems are solved in this way.

36 — Redefine a feature of one figure as a feature of another figure.

Consider next another example:

Question 2-38

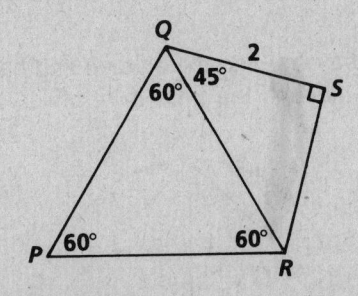

What is the perimeter of triangle PQR?

(A) $2\sqrt{3}$ (B) $3\sqrt{2}$ (C) 6 (D) $6\sqrt{2}$ (E) 12

What is required for a solution is not difficult to formulate. To find the perimeter of PQR we must know the length of each side:

Perimeter = PQ + QR + RP

The only length given is that for QS. QSR is an isosceles right triangle, so:

$$2^2 + 2^2 = QR^2$$
$$QR^2 = 8$$
$$QR = 2\sqrt{2}$$

QR is not only the hypotenuse of QRS, it is also one side of equilateral triangle PQR. So the perimeter of PQR must be:

$$3 \times 2\sqrt{2} = 6\sqrt{2}$$

and (D) is the correct answer.

Sometimes the test writers include a geometry problem with no figure. Without an illustration, it may be difficult to see how the given information is to be matched to the solution statement.

37 — If no figure is provided, sketch one yourself.

Question 2-39

An isosceles right triangle is inscribed in a circle. What is the ratio of the area of the circle to the area of the triangle?

(A) $\frac{1}{\pi}$ (B) 1   (C) π (D) 2π (E) $2\sqrt{2}\pi$

Our solution will be:

$$\frac{\text{Area of Circle}}{\text{Area of Triangle}} = \frac{\pi r^2}{\frac{1}{2}ab}$$

But we need the radius of the circle and the altitude and base of the triangle. Seeing a picture of the triangle inscribed in the circle is helpful:

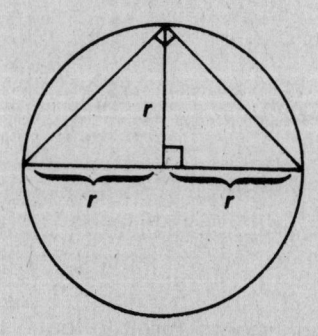

The diameter of the circle is also the base of the triangle, and the radius of the circle is the altitude of the triangle. Using r to designate the radius of the circle, we fill in our solution statement:

$$\frac{\text{Circle}}{\text{Triangle}} = \frac{\pi r^2}{\frac{1}{2}(r)(2r)} = \pi$$

So the correct answer is (C).
  Sometimes an incomplete figure will be provided.

38 If the figure is incomplete, sketch in the needed lines.

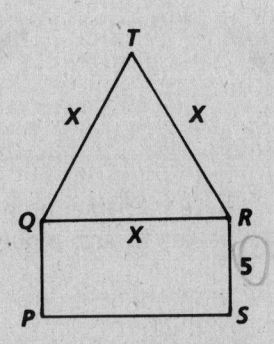

Question 2-40

In the figure above, the area of the rectangle is 50. What is the area of triangle QTR?

(A) 25   (B) $25\sqrt{3}$ (C) 30   (D) $30\sqrt{3}$ (E) $50\sqrt{3}$

The correct answer to this question is (B). To compute the area of equilateral triangle QTR, we need an altitude.

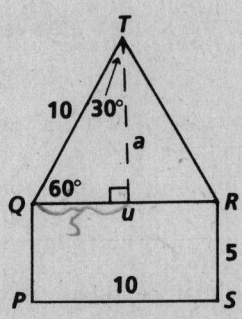

Since the area of PQRS is 50 and the width is 5, the length of PQRS must be 10. QR, therefore, equals 10, but QR is also the base of the triangle. Since QTR is equilateral, QT is also 10. The altitude forms one side of a 30:60:90 triangle, QTU, so TU, the altitude, is equal to $5\sqrt{3}$. Now we are in a position to find the area:

$$\text{Area} = \frac{1}{2}(5\sqrt{3})(10) = 25\sqrt{3}$$

48 | *101 Tips for Scoring High on the GMAT*

Now we discuss a different type of question. There are some geometry problems in which the solution statement is not so obvious. Consider the following example:

Question 2-41

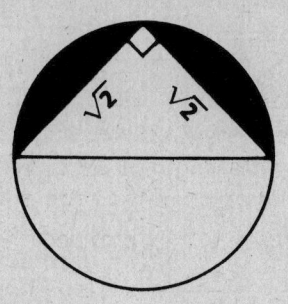

In the figure above, a right triangle is inscribed in a circle. What is the area of the shaded portion of the figure?

(A) 2π (B) $2\pi - 1$ (C) $2\pi - 2$ (D) $\pi - 1$ (E) $\pi - 2$

In this case, the shaded area is bounded by a figure that looks like this:

But this is a figure for which we have no name, no memorized formula and so no ready-made solution statement. The key to such a question is:

---
39 | The area of an irregular figure may be seen to be the difference between or the sum of the areas of two common, regular figures.

In this case, we can analyze the shaded area as being the difference between the semicircle and the triangle:

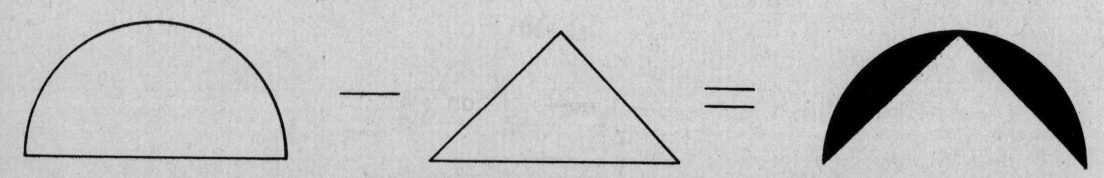

Expressed algebraically rather than pictorially, the solution statement is:

$$\frac{\pi r^2}{2} - \frac{1}{2}ab$$

We can use the two sides of the right triangle as altitude and base:

$$\frac{\pi r^2}{2} - \frac{1}{2}(\sqrt{2})(\sqrt{2})$$
$$\frac{\pi r^2}{2} - 1$$

Next we will redefine the radius of the circle in terms of the side of the triangle. The hypotenuse of the right triangle has length of $2\sqrt{2}$, and that is also the measure of the diameter of the circle. So the radius of the circle is $\sqrt{2}$:

$$\frac{\pi(\sqrt{2})^2}{2} - 1$$
$$\pi - 1$$

The correct answer is (D).

In the preceding example, we analyzed the shaded area as the difference between two known figures. Conversely, an irregular figure may sometimes be seen to contain two regular figures within it. Consider the following example:

Question 2-42

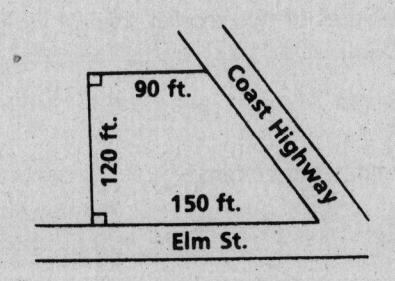

The figure above shows a piece of property with two street frontages. What is the area of the property in square feet?

(A) 7,200
(B) 10,800
(C) 14,400
(D) 18,000
(E) It cannot be determined from the information given.

Some readers will recognize that the property is a trapezoid and will recall that the formula for the area of such a figure is:

Average of Bases × Altitude

This special formula is not really necessary. The property can be seen to consist of two familiar figures, a rectangle and a triangle.

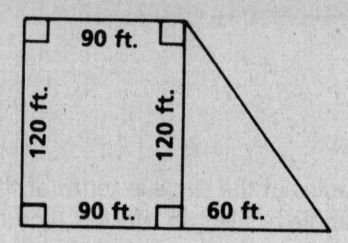

Expressed algebraically, our solution statement is:

$$\begin{aligned}\text{Area Rectangle} &+ \text{Area Triangle} &=& \text{Area of Property}\\ (120 \text{ ft.} \times 90 \text{ ft.}) &+ \tfrac{1}{2}(120 \text{ ft.})(60 \text{ ft.}) &=& \text{Area of Property}\\ 10{,}800 &+ 3{,}600 &=& 14{,}400 \text{ sq. ft.}\end{aligned}$$

The idea described in Key 39 may be extended to solid figures such as cylinders and spheres, and the key to such questions is:

---

40 — An irregular volume can be analyzed as the difference between the volumes of two regular solids.

The following problem illustrates the point:

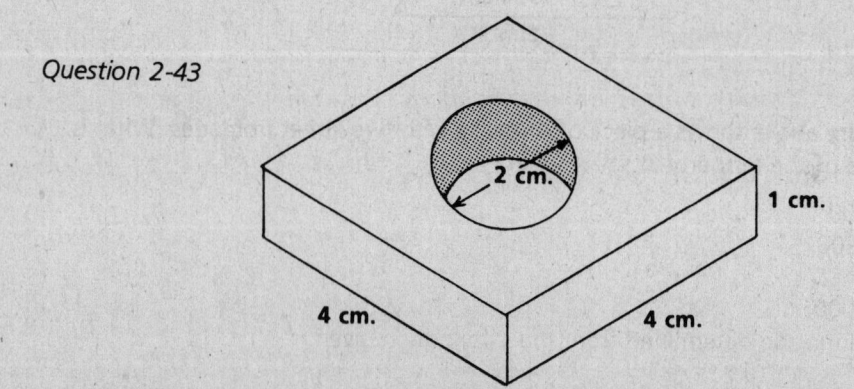

Question 2-43

The figure above shows the dimensions of a metal part made by boring a hole 2 centimeters in diameter through a solid rectangular piece of metal. After processing, how many cubic centimeters of metal are contained in the part?

(A) $8 - \pi$ (B) $9 - \pi$ (C) $8 + \pi$ (D) $16 - \pi$ (E) $16 + \pi$

The correct answer is (D), and the key is to see the finished part as a rectangular solid minus a cylindrical hole:

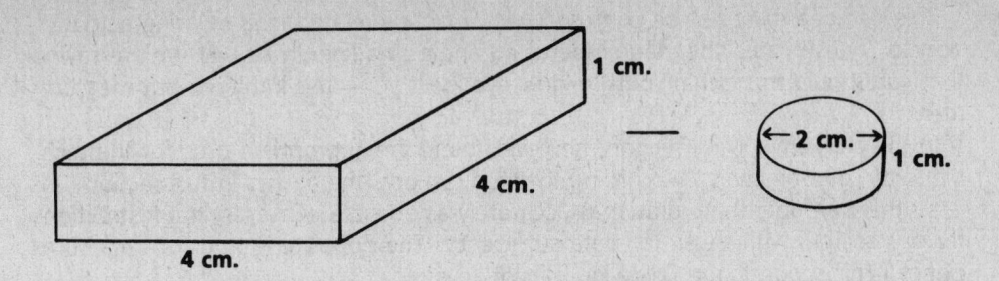

Problem Solving | 51

(length × width × height) − (π × radius² × height)
(4 × 4 × 1) − (π (1²)(1))
16 − π

With a little imagination you can see other variations on this theme are possible; for example, a ball in a box (sphere in cube) or a ball in a can (sphere in cylinder). The key to questions involving irregular volumes is to formulate a solution statement in which the irregular volume is defined as the difference between two regular solids.

What do you do if you cannot solve the problem using your knowledge of geometry?

First:

41 Trust your spatial intuition.

You must learn to recognize the difference between not having some important piece of knowledge about geometry and having the knowledge but not being able to present it in a formal way. Consider the following figure:

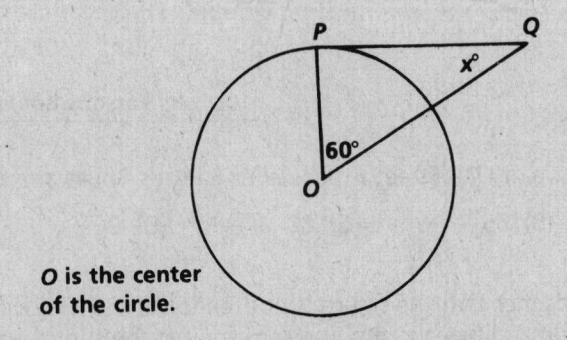

O is the center of the circle.

How many degrees are there in x? The answer is 30°, since angle P is a right angle. Most people will recognize this intuitively even though they may not be able to recite the formula: A radius that intersects a tangent at the point of tangency creates a right angle.

Thus we are often able to make correct judgments about geometry figures even though we cannot offer formal justifications for them. Given that, we urge strongly that if you have a hunch about a figure, play it. Chances are that your hunch will turn out to be correct.

This last idea must not be confused with a closely related idea of using actual vision to "guestimate" the magnitude of an angle or a line. In Key 41 we are saying that you should trust what your "mind's eye" tells you—use intuition, not measurement.

In the problem-solving section, however, there are appropriate uses for the technique of "guestimation." According to the directions, the figures in this section (unless otherwise noted) are drawn as accurately as possible. (Contrast the instructions for this section with those for data sufficiency. The opposite is true for data sufficiency.) This suggests the following pair of keys:

42 — Rely on your vision to "guestimate" the magnitude of angles, lines, and areas.

43 — Beware of figures accompanied by the legend: "*Note:* Figure Not Drawn To Scale."

Consider the following example:

Question 2-44

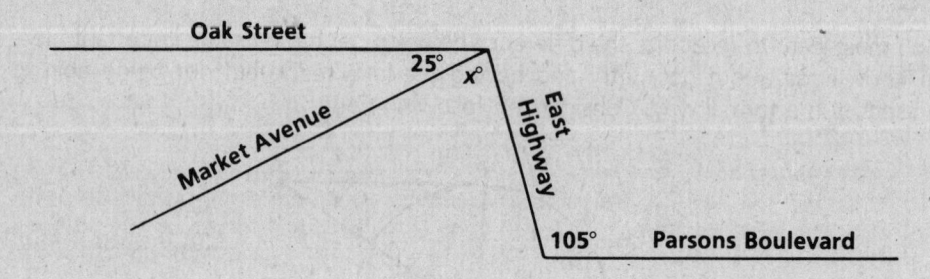

In the figure above, if Oak Street is parallel to Parsons Boulevard, then $x =$

(A) 45°   (B) 65°   (C) 80°   (D) 90°   (E) 105°

Since there is no disclaimer that the figure is not rendered to scale, we are entitled to rely on the relative magnitudes in the drawing. Look at the size of angle x. Is x as large as a right angle? No, so we eliminate both (D) and (E) as possible choices. Angle x is slightly smaller than 90°, but only slightly smaller, so our correct answer must be (C) rather than (A) or (B).

The correctness of (C) can be demonstrated mathematically. Since Oak Street and Parsons Boulevard are parallel, the angles of intersection between East Highway and Oak Street must equal 105°. Subtracting the 25° shown, the angle of intersection of Market Avenue and East Highway must be 80°. So $x = 80°$.

The corollary to this key is that you must not rely on figures accompanied by the disclaimer, "*Note*: Figure Not Drawn To Scale." Consider the following example:

Question 2-45

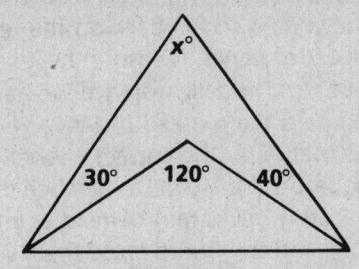

What is x?

(A) 40° (B) 50° (C) 60° (D) 90° (E) 120°

The figure in Question 2-45 is accompanied by the note warning that the figure is not drawn to scale. Therefore, you should not rely on the technique of "guestimation." You will have to use your knowledge of geometry to solve the problem.

The correct answer is (B). We know that the sum of the interior angles of the smaller triangle must be 180°. One of those angles is 120°, so the *sum* of the two unlabeled angles is 60°. Similarly, the angles of the larger triangle must total 180°. The *sum* of the two angles of the base of the larger triangle is: 60° + 40° + 30° = 130°. Angle x, therefore, must be 50°, and (B) is the correct answer.

The technique of "guestimation" must be used advisedly; and even in those cases where the technique is applicable, there is the danger of careless estimation. You can bring greater accuracy to your estimations of measurements with the following key:

Use your answer sheet as a ruler for measuring distances.

Your answer sheet is not attached to the test booklet, so it can be used as a measuring device. Admittedly, the answer sheet is not calibrated in units such as centimeters or inches, but you really have no need of such units. You are concerned only with the relative or scaled distances within the figure. Consider the following example:

Question 2-46

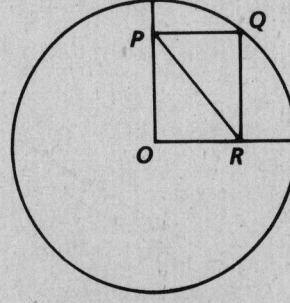

OPQR is a rectangle.

In the figure above, if the radius of Circle O is 1, what is the length of PR?

(A) π (B) 2 (C) 1 (D) $\frac{1}{2}$ (E) $\frac{1}{3}$

One way of solving *Question 2-46* is to see that *PR* is the diagonal of Rectangle *OPQR*. Since both diagonals of a rectangle have the same length, *PR* is equal to *OQ*. *OQ* is also the radius of the circle, so *PR* is equal to the radius, or 1.

If this insight eluded you, you could fall back on the technique of measuring. For practice, take a separate sheet of paper. Measure the length of *PR*, marking the distance on the edge of the paper. The only distance we have to compare *PR* to is the radius of the circle. So compare the marked distance with the radius of the circle: they are equal! This shows that (C) is the correct answer.

When using this technique on the exam, remember that your answer sheet will be machine graded and that stray marks may be read as intended responses. So make your measuring marks lightly and be sure to erase them when you have finished the question. Also check at the end of the exam to be sure you have not left stray marks on the answer sheet.

Not all distances will be integral values, so you should be prepared to make an approximation if necessary:

Question 2-47

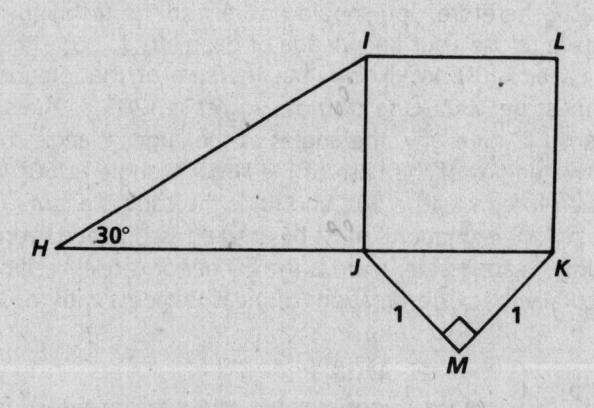

If *IJKL* is a square, what is the length of *HI*?

(A) 2   (B) $2\sqrt{2}$ (C) $2\sqrt{3}$ (D) 4   (E) $4\sqrt{2}$

If you measure carefully, using 1.4 as an approximation for $\sqrt{2}$ and 1.7 as an approximation for $\sqrt{3}$, you should be able to establish (B) as the correct answer. Begin by marking the distance of *JM*, 1, on the edge of your paper. Then compare that distance with the length of *HI*:

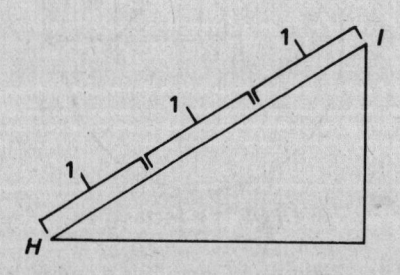

HI is between 2 and 3 times longer than 1. Checking the choices, we eliminate (A) as too small and (D) and (E) as too large. Then we use 1.4 and 1.7 for $\sqrt{2}$ and $\sqrt{3}$, respectively. (B) is approximately 2.8 and (C) is approximately 3.4. (B) must be the correct answer.

Since it is possible to measure distances, it may also be possible to find the area of a figure by measuring:

Question 2-48

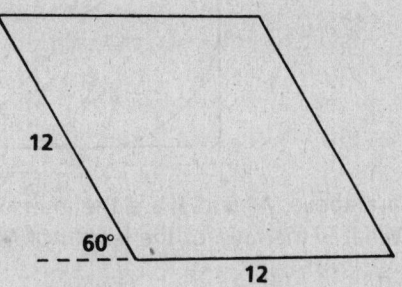

In the figure above, the area of the rhombus is

(A) 24 (B) $36\sqrt{3}$ (C) 72 (D) $72\sqrt{3}$ (E) 144

The correct answer is (D). The formula for the area of any parallelogram (including an equilateral parallelogram or rhombus) is altitude times base. We begin by sketching the altitude:

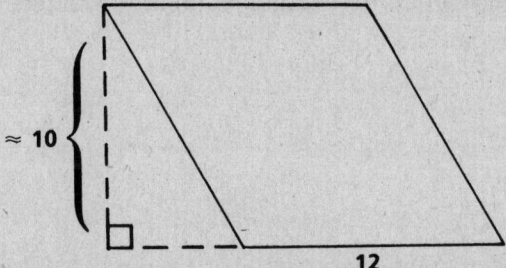

Now if you measure the altitude with the edge of your paper, and compare that distance with the known value of 12, you will find that it is approximately 10 units long. So the area of the figure must be approximately 120 square units. (C) is too small and (E) is too large, proving that (D) is the correct answer. And if further precision were required, you could have used 1.7 as an approximation for $\sqrt{3}$. Then (D) turns out to be $72 \times 1.7 = 122.4$, and the closest number to 120. We come now to our final key:

45 — When all else fails, eliminate any impossible choices and guess.

We have already emphasized the importance of using common sense to eliminate possible choices in other contexts. Now we apply this advice to geometry problems:

Question 2-49

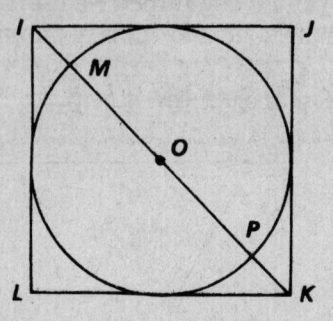

In the square above, M and P are the intersections of IK and the circle with center O. What is the ratio of the length of MP to the length of IK?

(A) $\sqrt{2} - 1$ (B) $\frac{\sqrt{2}}{2}$ (C) $\sqrt{2}$ (D) $\sqrt{2} + 1$ (E) $2\sqrt{2}$

The correct answer to *Question 2-49* is (B), and this can be justified by common sense. MP is shorter than IK, so the ratio of MP to IK must be less than 1. This eliminates (C), (D), and (E) as impossible answers. Next we compare (A) and (B). Using 1.4 as an approximation for $\sqrt{2}$, (A) is about .4 and (B) is about .7. Looking at the figure, we can see that MP is not less than half as long as IK, so the ratio of MP to IK must be greater than .5. This establishes (B) as the correct answer.

3.
DATA SUFFICIENCY

Data sufficiency is the "other" math section on the Graduate Management Admission Test (GMAT), the one section with the peculiar instructions:

DIRECTIONS

Each question below is followed by two numbered facts. You are to determine whether the data given in the statements is sufficient for answering the question. Use the data given, plus your knowledge of math and everyday facts, to choose between the five possible answers.

(A) if statement (1) alone is sufficient to answer the question, but statement (2) alone is not sufficient
(B) if statement (2) alone is sufficient to answer the question, but statement (1) alone is not sufficient
(C) if both statements together are needed to answer the question, but neither statement alone is sufficient
(D) if either statement by itself is sufficient to answer the question asked
(E) if not enough facts are given to answer the question

ABOUT DATA SUFFICIENCY QUESTIONS

Data sufficiency questions differ from other math questions such as problem-solving items in that you are not really expected to solve a math problem, as such. Rather, you are required only to determine whether or not the problem *could* be solved.

The question stems used in data sufficiency are usually of one of two general forms. There are those that require an exact numerical value for satisfaction:

> How much interest did the account earn in 6 months?
> What is the value of *x*?
> How many items are in a certain shipment?

There are also questions that require a yes or a no answer for satisfaction:

> Did the business make a profit in year 5?
> Is *x* greater than 0?
> Is the average age in a class more than 8 years?

The first is the more common form, but the second form appears with some frequency as well.

We will study each form and provide some illustrations. First:

---

46 — Information is considered sufficient to answer a question about numerical value only if the information produces a single unique value as an answer to the question.

In other words, if the question asks for a numerical value, it is not enough to give a range for the value or even to narrow the possibilities down to two.

---

47 — For a question that requires a numerical value for an answer, mark (A) if (1) alone provides the exact value needed but (2) alone does not.

For a question that requires a numerical value for an answer, mark (B) if (2) alone provides the exact value needed but (1) alone does not.

Consider the following examples:

Question 3-1

How many miles did Mary walk?

(1) Mary walked for 2 hours at an average rate of 3 miles per hour.
(2) Mary walked for one half hour after Bill stopped, and Bill walked 2 miles.

Question 3-2

What is the price of a single room for one night at the Hotel California?

(1) The price of a single room for one night at the Hotel California is less than the $50 charged by the Dew Drop Inn but more than the $40 charged by the Notell Motel.
(2) The price of a double room for one night at the Hotel California is $90, exactly twice the price of a single room.

3-1. (A) (1) alone is sufficient. If Mary walked for 2 hours at an average rate of 3 miles per hour, then she walked exactly 6 miles. That answers the question. (2) does not provide the rate at which Mary walked nor the time for which she walked. She and Bill may have walked at different speeds; and, insofar as we are told, they may not have started at the same time or from the same point.

3-2. (B) (2) is sufficient to establish that the price of the single room is half of the $90 price of a double, or $45. That answers the question. (1) is not sufficient. (1) fixes the price range between $40 and $50, but that range is not a sufficient answer to a question that asks for the exact price.

---

48 — For a question that requires a numerical value for an answer, mark (C) if neither (1) nor (2) alone provides the exact value needed but (1) and (2) together provide the exact value.

The following examples illustrate the point:

Question 3-3

What is the value of x?

(1) $x^2 = 4$
(2) x is positive.

Question 3-4

How much did Mary spend on theater tickets?

(1) She bought four tickets.
(2) Each ticket cost $25.

3-3. (C) (1) establishes that $x = \pm 2$, and that is not sufficient to answer the question. (2) establishes that $x > 0$, and that is not sufficient to answer the question. Both together are sufficient. (1) establishes that x is either $+2$ or -2, and (2) that x is positive, so $x = +2$.

3-4. (C) To determine exactly how much Mary spent on theater tickets, we need both the price of the tickets and the number of tickets purchased. So neither (1) nor (2) alone will be sufficient, but both taken together will tell us exactly how much Mary spent.

49 — For a question that requires a numerical value for an answer, mark (D) if (1) alone provides the exact value *and* (2) alone provides the exact value.

The following examples illustrate the point:

Question 3-5

What is the remainder when the positive integer x is divided by 2?

(1) x is an odd integer.
(2) y is an even integer, and $y = 3x + 1$.

Question 3-6

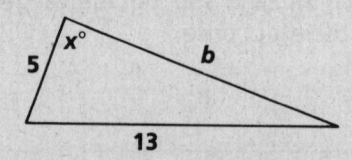

What is the area of the above triangle?

(1) $x = 90°$
(2) $5^2 + b^2 = 13^2$

3-5. (D) (1) is sufficient, for if x is an odd integer, when divided by 2, the result will be some quotient plus a remainder of 1; for example, $5 \div 2 = 2$ plus remainder 1. (2) is also sufficient, for if $3x + 1$ is equal to y, an even integer, then $3x + 1$ is itself an even integer, and $3x$ is an odd integer. But $3x$ can be an odd integer only if x is an odd integer. Again, if x is an odd integer, then the result when x is divided by two will be a quotient with a remainder of 1.

3-6. (D) (1) is sufficient to establish that the triangle is a right triangle, and using the Pythagorean Theorem we can compute the length of side b. Then we can use b and the side of 5 as an altitude and base to compute the area of the triangle. (2) is also sufficient. (2) is the Pythagorean Theorem, and any triangle that meets the conditions of the Pythagorean Theorem is a right triangle. Again, we know that x is a right angle, and we can solve for b, in turn using b and 5 to find the area of the triangle.

50 — For a question that requires a numerical value for an answer, mark (E) if both (1) and (2), even when taken together, do not provide an exact value.

The following examples illustrate the point:

Question 3-7

This year the enrollment of a certain school is 5 percent higher than last year. What is this year's enrollment?

(1) 180 students graduated last year.
(2) There are 38 new transfer students enrolled this year.

Question 3-8

What is the value of x?

(1) $x^4 = 16$
(2) $x^2 = 4$

Question 3-9

How many books can be packed into a shipping crate?

(1) The volume of the shipping crate is 24 cubic feet.
(2) The volume of each book is 144 cubic inches.

The correct answer to each question is (E).

3-7. (E) The question asks for the number of students enrolled this year. Even (1) and (2) together are not sufficient, for neither establishes last year's enrollment (which would give us this year's enrollment) and even both taken together do not give sufficient information to calculate this year's enrollment.

3-8. (E) There are two possible solutions to both equations, +2 and −2. The question, however, asks for the value of x, and that question cannot be satisfied by an answer of the form "x is this or that."

3-9. (E) Some crucial information is missing: the shape of the crate and the shape of the books. It is not sufficient just to divide the volume of the crate by the volume of each book, because the books may not fit neatly into the crate.

The other form of question is that which requires either a yes answer or a no answer:

> **51** Information is considered sufficient to answer a question eliciting a yes or a no response if and only if it provides a definite answer to the question one way or the other. Even a definite "no" response is a response.

Even a negative response is a definite response:

Question 3-10

Is x negative?

(1) x^3 is positive.
(2) $x^2 - 2x = -1$

3-10. (D) (1) establishes that *x* is positive, but if *x* is positive, we have a definite answer to the question: no, *x* is not a negative number. (2) also is sufficient to answer the question:

$$x^2 - 2x = -1$$
$$x^2 - 2x + 1 = 0$$
$$(x - 1)(x - 1) = 0$$
$$x - 1 = 0 \text{ or } x - 1 = 0$$
$$x = +1 \text{ or } x = +1$$

So $x = +1$. Since $x = +1$, the answer to the question is "no." The point is that a yes-or-no question is answerable when either a definite yes or a definite no is provided by the information. This situation does not occur very often on the test, but when it does it can be tricky. Some test takers confuse the negative response with "not sufficient," but even a negative answer is an answer.

52

For a question that elicits a yes or no response, mark (A) if (1) alone provides a definite answer to the question but (2) alone does not.

For a question that elicits a yes or no response, mark (B) if (2) alone provides a definite answer to the question but (1) alone does not.

Here are some examples:

Question 3-11

Is $x > y$?

(1) $x - y > 0$
(2) $x^2 > y^2$

Question 3-12

If *x* is an integer, is $\frac{x}{4}$ an *even* integer?

(1) *x* is a multiple of 4.
(2) *x* is a multiple of 8.

3-11. (A) This question requires a yes or no response. (1) is sufficient, for if $x - y > 0$, then *x* must be greater than *y*. (2) is not sufficient, for *x* might be negative and *y* positive; for example, $x = -4$ and $y = +2$, in which case $x < y$.

3-12. (B) (1) is not sufficient to answer the question, for there are some multiples of 4 for which $\frac{x}{4}$ is an even integer; for example, $x = 32$, and other multiples of 4 for which $\frac{x}{4}$ is an odd integer, for example, $x = 12$. So (1) does not supply a definite yes or a definite no answer. (2), however, does supply a definite answer. Since $8 = 2 \times 4$, if *x* is a multiple of 8, then $x = 2 \cdot 4 \cdot n$ where *n* is an integer. Thus, $\frac{x}{4} = 2n$, and $2n$ must be even, so $\frac{x}{4}$ must be even.

53 For a question that elicits a yes or no response, mark (C) if neither (1) nor (2) alone provides a definite answer to the question but (1) and (2) together do provide an answer.

Question 3-13

If two polygons, S and T, are each equilateral and equiangular, is the perimeter of S longer than that of T?

(1) Each angle of S is larger than each angle of T.
(2) Each side of S is longer than each side of T.

Question 3-14

Is the price of a pound of beans equal to the price of a pound of peas?

(1) The price of three ears of corn is equal to the sum of the price of a pound of peas and the price of a quart of milk.
(2) The sum of the price of a pound of beans and the price of a quart of milk is equal to the price of three ears of corn.

3-13. (C) Since these are regular polygons, (1) establishes that S has more sides than T, but it does not tell what the length of those sides is. So S might or might not have the longer perimeter. As for (2), it establishes that each side of S is longer than each side of T, but how many sides does each have? Both together establish that the perimeter of S is longer than that of T, for (1) establishes that S has more sides and (2) establishes that each of them is longer than each of T's sides.

3-14. (C) Neither (1) nor (2) alone is sufficient since neither, by itself, relates the price of beans to the price of peas. If we set both statements up as equations:

$$\text{corn} = \text{peas} + \text{milk}$$
$$\text{beans} + \text{milk} = \text{corn}$$

we see the possiblity of relating the price of peas to the price of beans:

$$\text{peas} + \text{milk} = \text{beans} + \text{milk}$$
$$\text{peas} = \text{beans}$$

The answer to the question is "yes, the two are equal," so we mark answer (C).

54 For a question that elicits a yes or no response, mark (D) if (1) alone provides a definite answer to the question *and* (2) alone provides a definite answer to the question.

The following questions illustrate the point:

Question 3-15

If $q \neq 0$, is $\frac{p}{q}$ an integer?

(1) $p = \sqrt{125}$ and $q = \sqrt{5}$
(2) $5q - p = 0$

Question 3-16

Mary and Bob both travel at constant rates, x kilometers per hour and y kilometers per hour, respectively. If they leave City X together and travel to City Y by the same route without stopping, does Mary arrive before Bob?

(1) $y > x$
(2) $x = 80$ and $y = 90$

Question 3-17

John and Phil each deposited exactly 50¢ per month into their respective piggy banks each month during a certain year, starting in January. If no withdrawals were made, which bank has more money in it at the end of the year?

(1) After the March deposit, John's bank contains exactly three times as much money as Phil's.
(2) After the June deposit, John's bank contains exactly twice as much money as Phil's.

The correct answer to each example is (D).
3-15. (D) (1) establishes that:

$$\frac{p}{q} = \frac{\sqrt{125}}{\sqrt{5}} = \sqrt{25} = 5$$

so x is positive.
(Do not confuse $x^2 = 25$, therefore $x = \pm\sqrt{25} = \pm 5$ with simply $\sqrt{25}$ which is $+5$. So (1) is sufficient.) (2) is also sufficient:

$$5q - p = 0$$
$$5q = p$$
$$5 = \frac{p}{q}$$

So $\frac{p}{q}$ is an integer, 5.

3-16. (D) (1) establishes that Bob arrives before Mary since he travels at the greater rate. Still, that is sufficient to answer the question definitely: "No, Mary does not arrive before Bob." (2) also is sufficient, for it too establishes that Mary does not arrive before Bob.

3-17. (D) This question does not, strictly speaking, have the yes/no format, but we will treat it as though it does; that is, we will consider the question "Who has the more money, John or Phil?" as asking "Does John have more money than Phil?"

Either (1) or (2) is sufficient. Each establishes that John has more money than Phil at some point during the year. Since money is added to each piggy bank at the same rate, John will always be ahead of Phil. To be sure, the ratio between the amounts changes. As the amounts grow, the ratio between them decreases, but the absolute difference remains the same.

> **55** For a question that elicits a yes or no response, mark (E) if both (1) and (2), even when taken together, do not provide a definite answer to the question.

The following examples illustrate the point:

Question 3-18

Is x greater than y?

(1) $1.25 < x < 1.45$
(2) $1.39 < y < 1.54$

Question 3-19

Is polygon P a square?

(1) P has four equal angles.
(2) The diagonals of P are equal.

Question 3-20

Did Glen receive a bigger raise than Ralph?

(1) Glen received a raise of 10 percent.
(2) Ralph received a raise of 5 percent.

3-18. (E) (1) establishes that x ranges between 1.25 and 1.45 and (2) establishes that y ranges between 1.39 and 1.54. It is possible that x is greater than y, but it is also possible that y is greater than x, or even that the two are equal.

3-19. (E) (1) and (2) taken together establish that P is a rectangle, but whether P is that special case of rectangle called a square is not known.

3-20. (E) Without knowing the original salaries (or resulting salaries), it is impossible to determine which person received the larger raise.

> **56** Become so familiar with the categories that you do not have to think about the underlying definitions.

By the time you take the test, you should be able to answer confidently without having to consult the directions.

A NOTE ABOUT GEOMETRY FIGURES

The geometry figures in this section are not necessarily drawn to scale.* A figure will conform to the information given in the question stem, but it will not necessarily conform to the additional information provided in the numbered statements. This means that the figure itself will not be sufficient to answer the question. It also means that you will have to use your knowledge of math, not your visual judgment, to solve questions.

*So the directions for data sufficiency are different from the directions for problem solving. In problem solving, unless otherwise indicated, figures are drawn to scale and "guestimation" is permitted. See Key 42.

57 | The apparent magnitude of angles, lines, and areas cannot answer the question asked.

The following examples illustrate the point:

Question 3-21

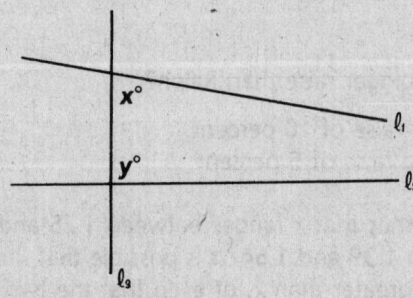

Are ℓ_1 and ℓ_2 parallel to each other?
(1) $x = y$
(2) $x + y = 180$

Question 3-22

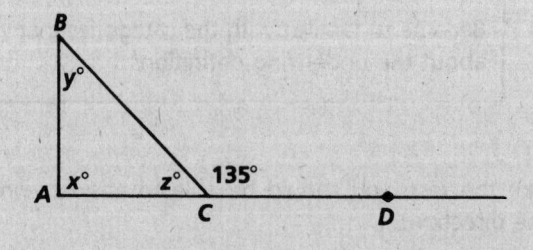

In the figure at the bottom of page 66, ABC is a triangle, and ACD is a straight line. What is the value of x?

(1) AB = AC
(2) y = z

Question 3-23

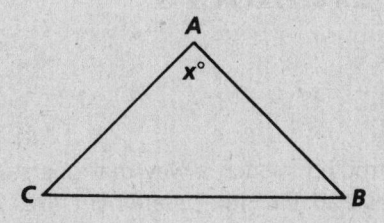

What is the value of x in the triangle above?

(1) BC = $\sqrt{2}$
(2) Angle ABC = 45°

3-21. (B) Although the lines do not appear to be parallel, you are not to draw any conclusion on the basis of their appearance. You know only that λ_1 and λ_2 are intersected by λ_3. (2) establishes that the lines are parallel; x and y are supplementary (total 180) only if the lines are parallel. (1) is not sufficient. If x = y = 90, the lines are parallel; but if x = y = 45, the lines are not parallel.

3-22. (D) Each statement establishes that x = 90. As for (1), z = 45, so if AB = AC, y = 45, which means that x = 90. As for (2), since z = y = 45, x = 90. We stress that we reach the conclusion that each statement establishes the value of x by mathematical reasoning, not by measuring angle x.

3-23. (E) Even assuming both (1) BC = $\sqrt{2}$ and (2) ABC = 45, it is not possible to establish the size of x.

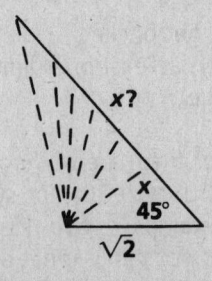

This further illustrates the importance of Key 57; you must not rely on the apparent magnitudes of the figure in determining the sufficiency of a statement. x does appear to be 90°, but even both statements together do not guarantee that as a matter of the principles of geometry.

COMMON PATTERNS

Now that we have discussed the general idea of sufficiency, we can introduce you to some of the common patterns used by the test writers.

Properties of Numbers

Integral Values

Some questions are constructed in such a way that one statement sets up a possible range of integer values and the other statement fixes one value within that range:

Key 58: For questions using quantities that come in integral values, look out for the possibility of a single, integral solution.

This key is illustrated by the following examples:

Question 3-24

Ellen put $1.30 in postage on a letter to be sent by certified mail. How many 20-cent stamps did she use?

(1) Ellen used only 15-cent and 20-cent stamps.
(2) Ellen used more than two 20-cent stamps.

Question 3-25

How many coins does Jura have in her pocket?

(1) She has exactly 44 cents in her pocket.
(2) She has at least one quarter, at least one dime, at least one nickel, and at least one penny in her pocket.

3-24. (C) (1) is not sufficient, for there are two possible mixes of stamps of those denominations that will total $1.30: two 20-cent stamps + six 15-cent stamps = $1.30 postage, and five 20-cent stamps + two 15-cent stamps = $1.30 postage. (2) is not sufficient because it does not tell us what other denominations were used. Both together are sufficient. (2) tells us which of the two possible arrangements Ellen used.

3-25. (C) (1) alone is not sufficient since many different combinations of coins will total 44 cents. Neither is (2) by itself sufficient, for it does not fix the total value of the coins. Both together are sufficient, for there is only one combination of the four coins that will total 44 cents:

1 quarter + 1 dime + 1 nickel + 4 pennies = 44 cents

Division Questions

Division questions ask you to determine some property of a number based on the result when that number is divided by some other value. For example:

Question 3-26

Is x an integer?

(1) $\frac{x}{3}$ is an integer.

(2) $\frac{x}{5}$ is not an integer.

3-26. (A) (1) is sufficient for it implies that x is a multiple of 3, and any multiple of 3 must be an integer. (2) is not sufficient, for (2) implies only that x is not a multiple of 5. But there are many numbers that are not multiples of 5, some integers, for example, 9, others not, for example $\frac{1}{3}$. Remember:

59 — If $\frac{x}{n}$ is an integer, where n is an integer, then x is an integral multiple of n.

A related type of question asks you to determine whether a certain number is odd or even:

Question 3-27

Is x an *even* integer?

(1) $\frac{x+x+x+x+x}{5}$ is an integer.

(2) $\frac{x+x}{4}$ is an integer.

3-27. (B) (1) is not sufficient, for $\frac{x+x+x+x+x}{5} = \frac{5x}{5} = x$ and that says only that x is an integer—not whether x is odd or even. (2), however, is sufficient, for $\frac{x+x}{4} = \frac{2x}{4} = \frac{x}{2}$. If $\frac{x}{2}$ is an integer, this means that x is a multiple of 2:

60 — If $\frac{x}{2n}$ is an integer, where n is an integer, this implies that x is a multiple of 2 and that x is even.

A similar question could be set up using the concept of remainder:

Question 3-28

What is the remainder when positive integer *p* is divided by 2?

(1) *p* is a multiple of 3.
(2) *p* is an odd integer.

3-28. (B) (1) is not sufficient, for multiples of 3 may be either odd or even; for example, 3 and 9 or 6 and 12. (2) is sufficient, for if *p* is odd, then when *p* is divided by 2, there will be a remainder of 1:

> **61** Division of the form $\frac{x}{2}$, where *x* is an odd integer, always results in a remainder of 1.

Finally, you should also remember that if a number is divisible by a second number, it is also divisible by any factor of the second number. Consider the following example:

Question 3-29

Is $\frac{x}{7}$ an integer?

(1) $\frac{x}{707,707}$ is an integer.
(2) $\frac{x}{123}$ is an integer.

3-29. (A) (1) is sufficient. 707,777 is divisible by 7, so if $\frac{x}{707,707}$ is an integer, then so too $\frac{x}{7}$ must be an integer. (2) is not sufficient. Since 123 is not divisible by 7, we can draw no conclusion about $\frac{x}{7}$. Even given statement (2), it is possible that *x* is divisible by 7; for example, if *x* = (707,707)(23), and it is possible that *x* is not divisible by 7; for example, if *x* = 123.

> **62** If *n* is a multiple of *m*, then, if $\frac{x}{n}$ is an integer, $\frac{x}{m}$ is also an integer.

Sequence

> **63** To find a particular term in a sequence, you must know (1) the rule for constructing the sequence, and (2) the value of some particular term of the sequence.

This type of question is illustrated by the following examples:

Question 3-30

What is the five hundredth term of S, a certain sequence of numbers?

(1) The first five terms of S are 1^3, 2^3, 3^3, 4^3, and 5^3.
(2) For every n, the nth term of S is n^3.

Question 3-31

What is the first term in sequence S?

(1) The fourth term is three more than the third term, the third term is twice the second term, and the second term is one and one-half times the first term.
(2) The fourth term of S is 8.

3-30. (C) (1) is not sufficient, for (1) does not give the rule for constructing the sequence. You cannot generalize on the first five terms and conclude that every term in the sequence is the cube of its position in the sequence. The pattern of (1) may not hold good after the first five terms. This is why (2) is needed. But (2) alone, the rule for constructing the sequence, is not sufficient, for we lack a point of reference. We cannot assume that the first term of the sequence is 1. It might be −1, 0, or 500. Both taken together, however, give us a rule for constructing the sequence and a point of reference.

3-31. (C) (1) is necessary but not sufficient to answer the question. (1) is the rule for constructing the sequence. (2) is needed for the point of reference it provides. (2) tells us the fourth term is 8. Using the rule provided by (1), we could then work backward to the first term in S. Note that in this question the point of reference is the fourth term—not the first.

Ratio and Percent

> **64** Given two quantities, x and y, if you know any one of the three relationships, what fraction one is of the other, what percent one is of the other, or the ratio between the two, you also know the other two relationships.

Consider the following examples:

Question 3-32

If $x > 0$, then x is what percent of y?

(1) $x = \frac{1}{5}y$

(2) The ratio of x to y is 1 to 5.

Question 3-33

How much money did Corporation X spend on air travel for its executives?

(1) Air travel accounted for $\frac{1}{12}$ of the corporation's travel expenditures, and travel expenditures accounted for $11\frac{1}{9}$ percent of the corporation's total expenditures of $360,000.

(2) Air travel accounted for $\frac{1}{36}$ of all of the corporation's expenditures.

3-32. (D) Since a percent is nothing more than a fraction written in a special way, (1) is sufficient. If $x = \frac{1}{5}y$, then x is $\frac{1}{5}$, or 20 percent of y. Similarly, if the ratio of x to y is 1 to 5, then $\frac{x}{y} = \frac{1}{5}$, and again, $x = \frac{1}{5}y$, or $x = 20$ percent of y. So (2), too, is sufficient.

3-33. (A) (1) is sufficient to determine what fraction of the total budget was spent on air travel; and that, when applied to the dollar figure for the total budget, will establish what amount was spent on air travel. (2) is not sufficient because no dollar figure is included.

Key 65: Given two quantities, x and y, if you know what fraction one is of the other, what percent one is of the other, or the ratio between the two, you also know the reciprocal of that relation.

Consider the following application of this principle:

Question 3-34

If $xy \neq 0$, what percent is y of x?

(1) x is 300 percent of y.
(2) $x = 3y$

3-34. (D) (1) is sufficient, for it establishes that $x = 3y$, and by simple manipulation, we determine that $y = \frac{1}{3}x$, so y is $33\frac{1}{3}$ percent of x. (2) also is sufficient for the same reason.

Key 66: Fractions, ratios, and percents do not provide information about actual quantities, only about the relationship between two quantities.

The following question shows how the exam writer might use this principle:

Question 3-35

Container P holds how many more quarts of liquid than container Q?

(1) If container Q were filled with liquid, and that liquid poured into P, which was empty, P would be ¾ full.
(2) Both containers together hold a total of 14 quarts.

3-35. (C) (1) is not sufficient. The question requires a numerical value, that is, the number of quarts. (2) alone is not sufficient, for it does not distinguish the capacity of P from that of Q. Both taken together are sufficient. (1) establishes that $Q = \frac{3}{4}P$, and (2) establishes that $P + Q = 14$. So $P = 8$ and $Q = 6$.

---

67 | A statement that provides the ratio (or some similar relationship) between two quantities is sufficient to determine which of the two is larger.

Consider the following examples:

Question 3-36

Is it cheaper to buy pencils by the gross than singly?

(1) The cost of a single pencil is $\frac{1}{144}$ the cost of a gross of pencils.
(2) A gross of pencils costs $5.76.

Question 3-37

Which of three children, X, Y, or Z, is the youngest?

(1) X's age is $\frac{2}{3}$ of Y's age.
(2) Z's age is $\frac{5}{4}$ of X's age.

3-36. (A) Although (1) gives only a relationship between the two quantities in question, and not their numerical values, (1) is sufficient to answer the question. (1) establishes that the cost of a single pencil is $\frac{1}{144}$ the cost of 144 pencils, that is, the costs are the same. So (1) answers the question with a definite negative: it's not cheaper. Still, that is an answer, so (1) is sufficient. (2) is not sufficient.

3-37. (C) Neither statement provides the age of the three individuals, but both statements taken together do establish that X is the youngest. (1) establishes that X is younger than Y. (2) establishes that Z is older than X, and therefore, X must be younger than Z.

---

68 | A change in actual quantities may change a known ratio into an unknown ratio.

Consider the following example:

Question 3-38

If the ratio of girls to boys at School S in 1983 was ⅔, what was the ratio of girls to boys at the school in 1984?

(1) 25 more boys were enrolled in S in 1984 than in 1983.
(2) 25 more girls were enrolled in S in 1984 than in 1983.

3-38. (E) Do not be fooled by the fact that the increase in the number of boys and the increase in the number of girls were both 25 students. The new ratio is unknown. If there were originally 50 students in the school, 20 girls and 30 boys, in 1984, the ratio of girls to boys was 45:55 or 9:11. If there were originally 100 students in the school, 40 girls and 60 boys, then in 1984, the ratio of girls to boys was 65:85 or 13:17.

---

69 — A statement about percentage change alone does not provide information about actual quantities.

Consider an example:

Question 3-39

Whose salary is larger, Jane's or Bob's?

(1) Jane received a salary increase of 15 percent.
(2) Bob received a salary increase of 10 percent.

3-39. (E) Although we know the percentage increase in the salary of each, we still have no information about the numerical value of the salaries. Without that information, we cannot answer the question which asks which salary is larger.

---

70 — Information about the percentage change and the resulting new value is sufficient to calculate the original value.

Consider this example:

Question 3-40

What was the cost of a certain train ticket in 1983?

(1) The price of the ticket increased by 25 percent from 1983 to 1984.
(2) In 1984, the ticket cost $25.00.

3-40. (C) Neither statement alone is sufficient to answer the question. (1) gives just the percentage change, not the value. (2) gives the new value, but makes no reference to change. Both together do provide an answer to the question:

$$\frac{1984 \text{ Price} - 1983 \text{ Price}}{1983 \text{ Price}} = \text{Percentage Change}$$

$$\frac{25 - x}{x} = .25$$

This is an equation with only one unknown, so it is possible to find the exact value of the old price.

Algebra

Algebraic expressions use letters called unknowns or variables, and these letters, unless otherwise restricted, can represent any number, positive, negative, or zero. Because of this, algebraic expressions and equations appear on the exam with great frequency.

> **71** Unless otherwise restricted, an unknown ranges over the entire number line.

The most important values to keep in mind are the negative numbers, zero, fractions, positive one, and numbers greater than positive one. Why? Because each of these values has identifiable properties that the test writer can use.

> **72** For negative numbers, the larger the absolute value of the number, the smaller the actual value.

As the negative numbers get "bigger," for example, from -2 to -7, they actually get smaller, -2 is greater than -7. Consider an example that tests your ability to appreciate this:

Question 3-41

If $pq \neq 0$, is $p > q$?

(1) $3p = 4q$
(2) $p > 0$

3-41. (C) (1) is not sufficient because of the possibility of negative values for p and q. (1) does establish that $q = \frac{3}{4}p$, but that does not mean that p is necessarily larger than q. If p is -8, then q is -6, but -6 is greater than -8. Of course, if p and q

are positive, then p is larger; for example, $p = 8$ and $q = 6$. (2), though not in and of itself sufficient, establishes that p is greater than 0. So both statements taken together establish that p and q are positive, so p is larger than q.

73. Beware of a variable raised to a power.

Consider the following example:

Question 3-42

Is $ab < 0$?

(1) $ab^2 > 0$
(2) $a^2b^3 < 0$

3-42. (C) (1) alone is not sufficient, even though it does establish that a is positive. b^2 cannot be zero. If b^2 were zero, then (1) would be $ab^2 = 0$. Since $ab^2 > 0$, b^2 has a positive value. By the same reasoning a must be positive. This does not establish whether b, as opposed to b^2, is positive or negative. (2) alone is not sufficient. It does establish that b is negative, though it says nothing about whether a is positive or negative. We know that b must be negative because b^3 must be negative. Both statements together establish that a is positive and b is negative, and this is sufficient to answer the question.

74. The product of 0 and any number is 0. The product of any number and 1 is that number. The sum of 0 and any number is that number.

Consider the following examples:

Question 3-43

* represents either multiplication or addition. What does * represent?

(1) $x * 0 = x$
(2) $0 * 0 = 0$

Question 3-44

What is the value of $x^2 - y^2$?

(1) $x - y = 0$
(2) $x = 10$

3-43. (A) * represents either multiplication or addition. Statement (1) establishes that it represents addition, for when 0 is added to any value the result is the original value. If * represented multiplication, then $x * 0 = 0$. (2) is not sufficient, for $0 \times 0 = 0$ and $0 + 0 = 0$.

3-44. (A) (1) is sufficient. $x^2 - y^2 = (x + y)(x - y)$. If $x - y = 0$, the entire expression has the value 0. (2) is neither sufficient nor necessary.

---

75 — An equation with variables raised to a power may have more than one solution.

Consider the following example:

Question 3-45

What is x?

(1) $x^2 - 1 = 0$
(2) $x > 0$

3-45. (C) (1) alone is not sufficient because there are two possible solutions to the equation:

$$x^2 - 1 = 0$$
$$(x + 1)(x - 1) = 0$$

So either $x + 1$ or $x - 1$ is zero, which means that x is either -1 or $+1$. (2) is needed, then, to specify which of the solutions is to be considered the value of x. (2) establishes that x is positive, so both (1) and (2) together establish x as $+1$.

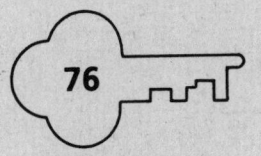

---

76 — Be alert to the possibility that the two statements function as simultaneous equations.

Question 3-46

What is x?

(1) $x + y = 6$
(2) $y = 2x$

Question 3-47

What is x?

(1) $xy = 10$
(2) $x - y = 3$

3-46. (C) Neither statement alone is sufficient because each is an equation containing two variables. Both statements taken together, however, can function as simultaneous equations. (2) establishes that $y = 2x$, so we can substitute $2x$ for y in the equation in (1): $x + (2x) = 6$, so $x = 2$. y, therefore, is equal to 4.

3-47. (E) Not all attempts to combine equations will result in one set of solutions. In this example, even treating the two statements as simultaneous equations does not fix the value of x. Using the equation in (2), we solve for x: $x = y + 3$, and we substitute this into the first equation:

$$(y + 3)y = 10$$
$$y^2 + 3y - 10 = 0$$
$$(y + 5)(y - 2) = 0$$

So either $y = -5$ or $y = +2$, and either $x = -2$ or $x = +5$. Since we have two solution sets, we cannot give an exact value for x, so the answer is (E). (See also above, for another look at simultaneous equations.)

---

77 If a question asks for the value of a complex algebraic expression, try to simplify the expression.

Question 3-48

If $xy \neq 0$, what is the value of $\dfrac{x^5y^3 - (xy)^3}{x^4y^3}$?

(1) $x = 3$
(2) $y = 4$

3-48. (A) At first glance, it appears that both (1) and (2) are necessary because the expression we must evaluate contains both x and y terms. A closer look shows that the y terms cancel out:

$$\dfrac{x^5y^3 - (xy)^3}{x^4y^3} = \dfrac{x^5y^3 - x^3y^3}{x^4y^3} = \dfrac{y^3(x^5 - x^3)}{x^4y^3} = \dfrac{x^5 - x^3}{x^4}$$

The y term drops out leaving only the x term. (1) alone is sufficient, and the answer is (A).

To simplify an expression, use the standard algebraic techniques of manipulating exponents and factoring. There is one factoring tool that is particularly useful on the exam:

---

78 When you see an algebraic expression that is the difference between two squares, factor it.

Consider the following examples:

Question 3-49

What is the value of $x^2 - y^4$?

(1) $x + y^2 = 3$
(2) $x - y^2 = 2$

Question 3-50

What is the value of $x^4 - y^4$?

(1) $x^2 + y^2 = 0$
(2) $x^2 - y^2 = 5$

Each of the examples is solved by recognizing that the expression to be evaluated is the difference between two squares. The general form for such an expression is $x^2 - y^2$, and it can be factored as $(x + y)(x - y)$.

3-49. (C) Since x^2 is a square (the square of x) and y^4 is a square (the square of y^2), $x^2 - y^4$, the difference between two squares, can be factored: $(x + y^2)(x - y^2)$. (1) gives the value of just the first factor. (2) gives the value of just the second factor. So neither alone is sufficient. But both taken together establish that the value of $x^2 - y^4$ is $(3)(2) = 6$.

3-50. (A) Since x^4 is a square (the square of x^2) and y^4 is a square (the square of y^2), $x^4 - y^4$ is the difference between two squares and can be factored: $x^4 - y^4 = (x^2 + y^2)(x^2 - y^2)$. (2) alone is not sufficient since it requires a value for the first factor. (1) alone, however, is sufficient. If one of the two factors is zero, then the value of the entire expression must also be zero. See Key 74.

Geometry Questions

Many of the questions that are built on the principles of geometry take advantage of the logical and mathematical properties of special geometry figures such as circles, squares, or equilateral triangles. Let us review some of the most important principles of such figures beginning with triangles.

You will surely recall the Pythagorean Theorem: the square of the hypotenuse is equal to the sum of the squares of the other two sides. Thus, if you have a right triangle and know any two of the sides, it is possible to calculate the remaining side:

> **79** If a triangle is a right triangle, look for the possibility of using the Pythagorean Theorem.

The use of the Theorem should be familiar to you from our discussion in Chapter 2, but there is a data sufficiency twist to be alert for:

80

Any triangle that fits the Pythagorean Theorem is a right triangle.

Thus, consider:

Question 3-51

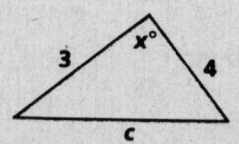

What is the value of x in the figure above?

(1) $c^2 = 3^2 + 4^2$
(2) $c = 5$

3-51. (D) (1) is sufficient since it asserts that the triangle satisfies the Pythagorean Theorem, so the triangle is a right triangle and x must be a right angle. (2) is also sufficient, for it too establishes that the triangle is a right triangle. Remember:

81

A triangle the sides of which are 3, 4, and 5 (or some multiple thereof such as 6, 8, and 10), is a right triangle.

You should also keep in mind those special cases of the right triangle, the 30:60:90 triangle and the 45:45:90 triangle. The sides of the 30:60:90 triangle are in the ratio $1:\sqrt{3}:2$. The sides of the 45:45:90 triangle are in the ratio $1:1:\sqrt{2}$.

82

Be alert for 30:60:90 and 45:45:90 triangles, for information about one side is sufficient to establish the other sides.

Consider:

Question 3-52

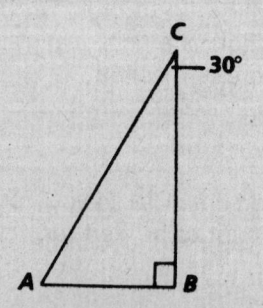

What is the length of AC in the triangle at the bottom of page 80?

(1) $AB = 1$
(2) $BC = \sqrt{3}$

Question 3-53

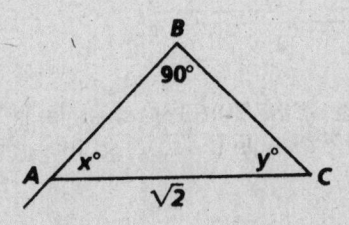

What is the length of AB in the triangle above?

(1) $AB = BC$
(2) $x = y$

3-52. (D) In a 30:60:90 triangle, the sides are in the ratio of $1:\sqrt{3}:2$. Knowing the length of any one side is sufficient information to allow the calculation of the others. (1), therefore, is sufficient since the hypotenuse must be double the side opposite the 30° angle. So $AC = 2$. (2) is sufficient as well. The side opposite the 60° angle is one half the hypotenuse times $\sqrt{3}$, so $AC = 2$.

3-53. (D) In a 45:45:90 triangle, the sides are in the ratio $1:1:\sqrt{2}$. (1) establishes that the two sides are equal, so $x = y$, and we have such a triangle. This means that $AB = 1$. Similarly, (2) directly establishes that $x = y$, so x and y must be 45°. Again, we know the length of AB.

Another special triangle is the equilateral triangle. It is related, in a way, to the 30:60:90 right triangle:

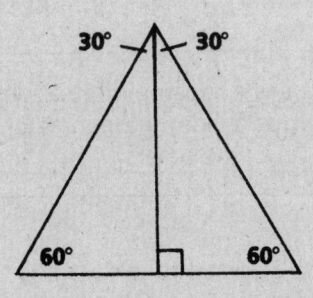

The altitude of an equilateral triangle divides the equilateral triangle into two equal 30:60:90 triangles. So:

83

If the triangle is equilateral, information about any one of the following: length of a side, the perimeter, the altitude, or the area, is sufficient to fix the other elements.

For example, if you know that the perimeter of an equilateral triangle is 6, you can calculate the area:

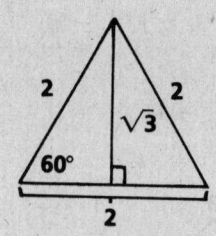

The side, which is the hypotenuse of the 30:60:90 triangle, is 2, so the altitude of the triangle is $\sqrt{3}$. The base of the triangle is also 2, so the area of the entire equilateral triangle is

$$\text{Area} = \tfrac{1}{2} \text{ altitude} \times \text{base}$$
$$A = \tfrac{1}{2}(\sqrt{3})(2) = \sqrt{3}.$$

This could easily be turned into a question in the data sufficiency format:

Question 3-54

What is the area of equilateral triangle *ABC*?

(1) Each side of triangle *ABC* is 2.
(2) The perimeter of triangle *ABC* is 6.

3-54. (D) As we have just shown, either statement alone is sufficient to determine the area of the triangle.

A square is related to the 45:45:90 triangle in much this fashion, for the diagonal of a square creates two equal isosceles right triangles:

84 If the figure is a square, information about any one of the following, length of a side, the perimeter, the diagonal, or the area, is sufficient to fix the others.

For example, if we know that the diagonal of a square is $\sqrt{2}$, we also know the length of each side is 1, the perimeter is 4, and the area is 1:

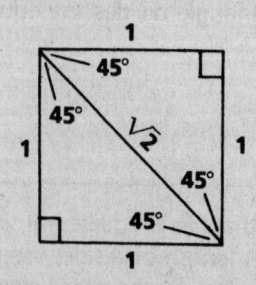

This can become the basis for a data sufficiency question:

Question 3-55

What is the length of the side of square *PQRS*?

(1) The diagonal of square *PQRS* is $4\sqrt{2}$.
(2) The number of units in the perimeter of *PQRS* is equal to the number of square units in the area.

3-55. (D) As we have shown, knowledge of the length of the diagonal is sufficient to permit a determination of the length of the side, so (1) is sufficient. (2) is also sufficient:

$$\text{Units in Perimeter} = \text{Units in Area}$$
$$4s = s^2$$
$$4 = s$$

So the length of side *s* is 4.

This principle could actually be carried to a higher level of difficulty and applied to a cube. A cube is just a three-dimensional square:

> 85 If the figure depicts a cube, information about any one of the following, length of a side, area of a face, length of diagonal of a face, length of diagonal of the cube, or volume, is sufficient to fix the others.

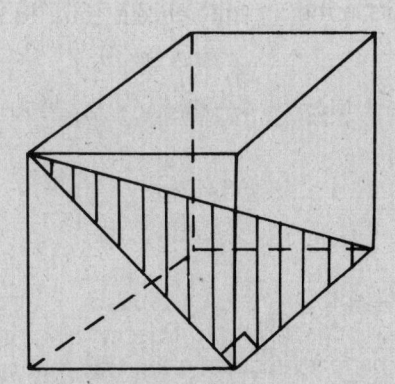

Each of the six faces of the cube is a square with the properties already mentioned. The volume of a cube is computed as (side × side × side). The one point that is perhaps not so easily seen is that the diagonal of the cube is a function of the length of the side as well. The diagonal of the cube runs from one corner to the opposite corner. This diagonal, plus one side of the cube, plus the diagonal of one of the faces makes a right triangle. If the cube has a side of 1, the diagonal of each face is $\sqrt{2}$, and these are two of the sides of the right triangle, the hypotenuse of which is the diagonal of the cube:

$$d^2 = (1^2) + (\sqrt{2})^2$$
$$d^2 = 1 + 2$$
$$d = \sqrt{3}.$$

Many people have difficulty with three-dimensional figures, and any question testing the properties we have just described would be one of the most difficult in the section. Just remember that knowing any one of the measurements is sufficient to determine the other measurements. And in the data sufficiency section you need only to recognize this, you do not actually have to perform the calculation.

A circle has features analogous to those of the equilateral triangle and the square:

> **86** If the figure is a circle, information about any of the following, radius, diameter, circumference, or area, is sufficient to fix the others.

If you know the diameter of the circle, you obviously know the radius, for the radius is half the diameter; and if you know the radius, then you can calculate the circumference ($C = 2\pi r$) and the area (πr^2). Conversely, if you know either the circumference or the area, you can find the radius of the circle. The following example shows how the test writer might use this information:

Question 3-56

What is the radius of circle O?

(1) The area of the circle is 4π.
(2) The number of units in the circumference is equal to the number of square units in the area.

3-56. (D) (1) is sufficient. If $\pi r^2 = 4\pi$, then $r = 2$. (2) is also sufficient:

$$\pi r^2 = 2\pi r$$
$$r = 2.$$

So each statement is sufficient.

You may encounter a cylinder in data sufficiency. Since cylinders can have different heights, they are not perfectly regular in the way that cubes are. Still, a little information can go a long way. First, knowing the radius and the height enables you to compute the volume and the surface area of the cylinder. To compute the volume, you find the area of the circle that forms the base of the cylinder and multiply that by the height of the cylinder: $\pi r^2 h$. Thus, a cylinder with a radius of 2 and a height of 5 has a volume of $\pi(2^2)5 = 20\pi$.

The surface area of the cylinder can be conceptualized as two discs, the bottom and the top, around which is wrapped a surface that is a rectangle:

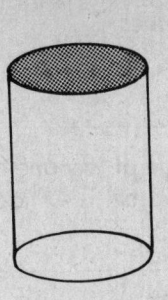

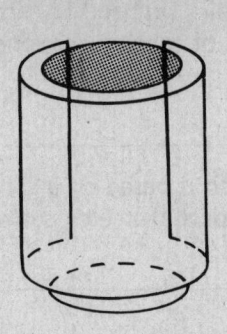

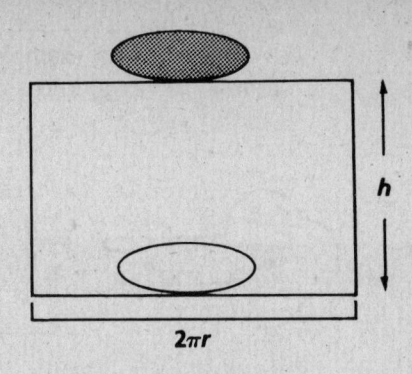

The area of each disc is πr^2. The area of the rectangular surface that is wrapped about them is length times width where the length is the circumference of the circle (the surface is wrapped around the circle) and the width is the height of the cylinder. So the formula for the area of a cylinder is: $2\pi r^2 + 2\pi r(h)$.

> **87** If the figure depicted is a cylinder, you need both the radius and the height to find volume or surface area. Conversely, given volume or surface area, you need to know the height to find the radius and vice versa.

Consider the following example:

Question 3-57

What is the volume of a right circular cylinder with a radius of 5?

(1) The total surface area of the cylinder, including top and bottom, is 150π.
(2) The height of the cylinder is 10.

3-57. (D) (2) is clearly sufficient. The question stem provides the radius, and (2) provides the height. (1) is also sufficient. The question stem establishes that the radius is 5, so the area of each end of the cylinder is $\pi r^2 = \pi(5^2) = 25\pi$. And since there are two ends, they account for 50π in area. The remaining area is the rectangular surface that forms the circular sides of the cylinder. Its area is the circumference of the circular end times the height:

$$100\pi = 2\pi r(h)$$
$$100\pi = 2\pi(5)(h)$$
$$h = 10$$

So (1) provides the height, and that when coupled with the radius given in the question stem is sufficient basis for determining the volume.

You might encounter a sphere in the data sufficiency section. In the past, when the GMAT has used a sphere in the problem-solving section, the needed formulas were provided; for example, Volume = $\frac{4}{3}\pi r^3$ and Surface Area = $4\pi r^2$. There is no reason for us to go into a discussion of spheres, for spheres are like cubes:

---

88 — If the question is based on a sphere, knowledge of any one of the following, radius, diameter, surface area, or volume, is sufficient to fix the others.

In other words, every aspect of a sphere is a function of one single measure: the radius.

There is one final technique that you may find useful.

---

89 — Try distorting a figure to learn the significance of the information provided by the numbered statements.

This is illustrated by the following examples:

Question 3-58

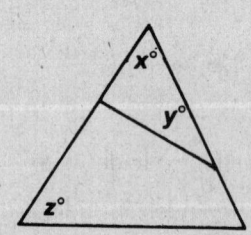

In the triangle above, what is the value of x?

(1) $y = 60$
(2) $z = 60$

Question 3-59

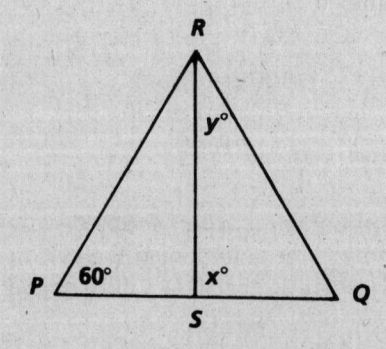

In the figure at the bottom of page 86, PQR is a triangle. What is the measure of angle PRS?
(1) x = 90
(2) y = 30

3-58. (E) Even using both statements, it is not possible to fix the value of x, as the following figures demonstrate:

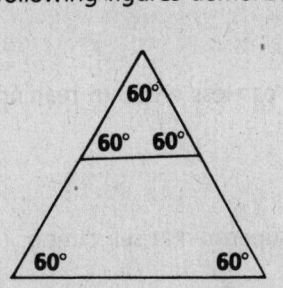

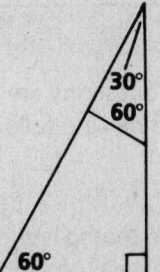

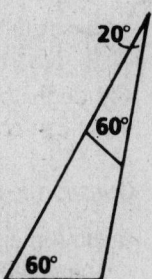

3-59. (A) That (2) alone is not sufficient is shown by the following figures:

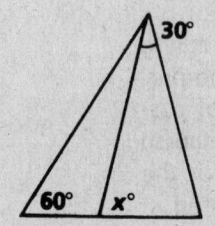

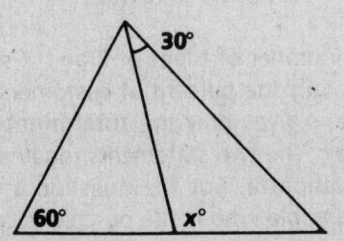

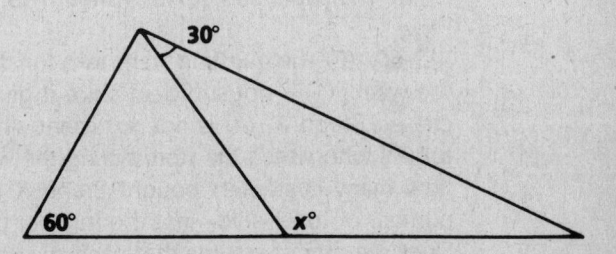

(1) is sufficient as a matter of mathematics:

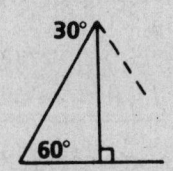

If x = 90, then PRS must equal 30.

DATA SUFFICIENCY ATTACK STRATEGY

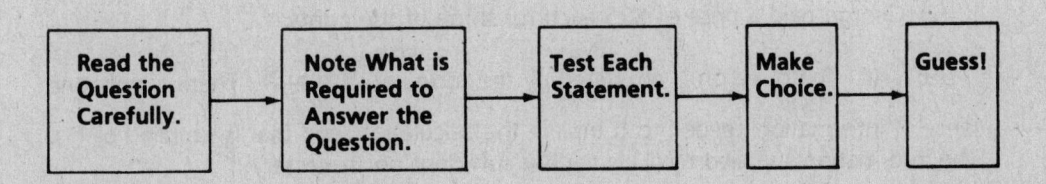

Read the Question Carefully. → Note What is Required to Answer the Question. → Test Each Statement. → Make Choice. → Guess!

The first step is:

> **90** Read the question carefully.

Although the data sufficiency questions are not lengthy, careless errors in reading them can cost you points. Consider the following example:

Question 3-60

How many tubes of Brand X toothpaste did a certain supermarket sell during the week?

(1) 18 percent of the customers who visited the supermarket purchased Brand X toothpaste.
(2) The supermarket was visited by 8,910 customers that week.

3-60. (E) The question stem asks for the number of tubes of Brand X sold during the week. (1) is not sufficient since it gives only the percent of customers who purchased Brand X. (2) is not sufficient since it gives only the total number of customers who visited the store during the week. The two statements together establish how many customers bought Brand X toothpaste. But the question asks for the number of tubes sold—not the number of people who made purchases of Brand X. Since we cannot assume that each customer who did purchase Brand X bought only one tube, we cannot answer the question asked.

The second step is to note exactly what is required to answer the question. If the question stem is more complex than a simple "What is x?" you may want to make a note of what is asked:

> **91** Make a note, in algebraic form if possible, of what the question requires.

Consider:

Question 3-61

George purchased four prints. What was the average price of the four prints?

(1) The total cost of the four prints was $120.
(2) George paid a price of $25 each for three of the prints.

3-61. (A) The question is answered by the formula: $\frac{\text{Total Cost}}{4}$. There is only one piece of information needed to complete the calculation, and that is supplied by (1). The information supplied by (2) is neither sufficient nor necessary.

When you are analyzing the question to ascertain exactly what is needed:

92 — Do not forget to use any information provided in the question stem.

Question 3-62

Sam and Cindy have $2,000 in their joint savings account. How much did each contribute?

(1) Sam contributed $500 less than Cindy.
(2) Cindy contributed three times as much as Sam.

3-62. **(D)** Let S and C represent the amounts contributed by Sam and Cindy, respectively. (1) establishes that $C - \$500 = S$, and (2) establishes that $C = 3S$. These two statements, without any additional information, could be used as simultaneous equations to answer the question asked. But there is no need to do so. The question stem gives the information: $C + S = \$2,000$. Now each statement alone, when coupled with this equation, answers the question. So the correct choice is not (C) but (D). The information provided in the question makes this difference.

The third step in attacking a data sufficiency question is to test each statement:

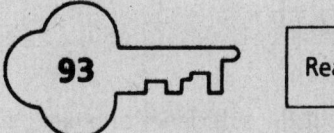

93 — Read each statement carefully.

Again, we stress the importance of careful reading. Consider the following example:

Question 3-63

How many miles did Sally run during a certain training run?

(1) If Sally had run exactly 1 mile more, she would have run a total of 8 miles on that run.
(2) If Sally had run for exactly 1 more hour, she would have run a total of 13 miles on that run.

3-63. **(A)** (1) establishes that Sally's actual total plus 1 mile is equal to 8, so the actual total was 7. (2) is not sufficient to answer the question, for (2) says that an extra *hour* of running would have resulted in a total of 13 miles. But you cannot subtract hours from miles. Since (2) provides information about time rather than miles, it is not sufficient.

94 — Test each statement independently, placing "✓" beside the statement if it is sufficient to answer the question and "X" if it is not sufficient.

It is very important that you consider the information provided by each statement, so you want to make sure that your study of a statement is not "contaminated" by something you have seen in the other statement. You may find it helpful to use your answer sheet or pencil to cover first one statement and then the other.

After you have studied the sufficiency of each statement, it may be possible to make your choice. Consider these possible situations:

$$\boxed{\begin{array}{l}\checkmark\ (1)\\ X\ (2)\end{array}} = (A) \qquad \boxed{\begin{array}{l}X\ (1)\\ \checkmark\ (2)\end{array}} = B \qquad \boxed{\begin{array}{l}\checkmark\ (1)\\ \checkmark\ (2)\end{array}} = (D) \qquad \boxed{\begin{array}{l}X\ (1)\\ X\ (2)\end{array}} \ (C)\ or\ (E)$$

This method of attack raises last the question of whether (1) and (2) are both necessary and sufficient to answer the question. That is sometimes a tricky question, so you should not begin to worry about the possible interaction of (1) and (2), (C), until you have determined that it is necessary to do so.

The final step in the attack strategy is this:

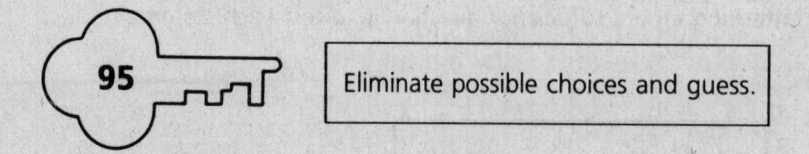

95 Eliminate possible choices and guess.

In this section, if you are able to make a determination about the sufficiency of either statement, you should guess. Consider the possibilities:

$$\boxed{\begin{array}{l}\checkmark\ (1)\\ (?)\ (2)\end{array}} = (A)\ or\ (D) \qquad \boxed{\begin{array}{l}(?)\ (1)\\ \checkmark\ (2)\end{array}} = (B)\ or\ (D)$$

$$\boxed{\begin{array}{l}X\ (1)\\ (?)\ (2)\end{array}} = (B),\ (C),\ or\ (E) \qquad \boxed{\begin{array}{l}(?)\ (1)\\ X\ (2)\end{array}} = (A),\ (C),\ or\ (E)$$

In each case you have eliminated two or three possible choices, so guess!

There is one final and very important principle to be observed in this section:

96 Do only as much work as is required to determine the sufficiency of the statements to answer the question.

Remember the task in this section is to assess the *sufficiency* of the statements, either singly or in conjunction, to answer the question. You should never do an actual calculation.

4.
ANALYSIS OF SITUATIONS

Analysis of situations is designed to measure your ability to understand the structure of a business or managerial situation by asking you to identify and classify the important elements of the situation; for example, the assumptions made by the decision maker about the situation, the goals the decision maker hopes will be realized, and the factors used by the decision maker to evaluate the available options. To a certain extent, the analysis of situations questions ask you to do something you do often in ordinary life. Daily life, after all, is filled with decisional situations, some simple and relatively insignificant (what to eat for breakfast or what movie to see), and others rather complicated and very important (what job to take or what model car to buy). Each such decision requires that you understand the situation you are in, set goals for yourself, and compare the available options in order to arrive at a choice.

The decisions described in the analysis of situations section differ in two respects from those you are accustomed to facing. First, the situations used by the Graduate Management Admission Test (GMAT) are likely to be unfamiliar to you; for example, what franchise restaurant to buy, how to store dangerous chemicals, where to build a new factory, what steam shovel to buy, how to finance the opera company. It is not that these decisions are any more complicated than the most complicated decisions you have already faced; it is just that they involve subject matter that is likely to be alien to you. This is one of the features of the section that makes it difficult.

A second complication is presented by the artificial test format. You will not be asked to make an actual decision. Instead, you will be asked to classify the various aspects of the hypothetical case according to a scheme set up by the GMAT.

DIRECTIONS

This section consists of reading selections which detail business situations. After each selection you will be asked to classify certain of the facts presented in the passage on the basis of their importance. Based on your analysis of the previous passage, classify each of the following items in one of five categories. Mark:

(A) if the item is a *Major Objective* in making the decision; that is, one of the outcomes or results sought by the decision maker.

(B) if the item is a *Major Factor* in making the decision; that is, a consideration, explicitly mentioned in the passage, that is basic in determining the decision.
(C) if the item is a *Minor Factor* in making the decision; that is, a secondary consideration that affects the criteria tangentially, relating to a major factor rather than to an objective.
(D) if the item is a *Major Assumption* in making the decision; that is, a supposition or projection made by the decision maker before weighing the variables.
(E) if the item is an *Unimportant Issue* in making the decision; that is, a factor that is insignificant or not immediately relevant to the situation.

The meanings intended by the definitions, however, are not entirely clear. Our approach to this section will first clarify the commonsense distinctions that underlie these definitions. Then we will study the directions more carefully to demonstrate that they do, indeed, have some basis in reality.

ANALYZING THE SITUATION

Perhaps the best way to learn the significance of the categories major objective, major/minor factor, and major assumption is to take a fairly simple decisional situation and analyze it using common sense. Then when we have a commonsense understanding, we will match that to the directions for the GMAT. The following decison is simple enough and should be somewhat familiar to you:

Stephen is on a one-day sightseeing trip in New York City, when the weather turns unseasonably cool. Stephen decides, therefore, to purchase a sweater. He goes into a large department store to visit the men's department. Stephen has $100 in traveler's checks and no cash or credit cards, so that amount must last him for the entire trip. Further, Stephan wears a man's size large, and his wardrobe at home is predominantly blue and gray.

At the sweater counter, Stephen finds three sweaters of the appropriate size: a solid gray, all-wool sweater for $32; a white, all-cotton sweater for $38; and a patterned, gray-and-blue acrylic sweater for 18.

Stephen would like to purchase the $18 sweater since it is the cheapest and that would leave him with more money for his sightseeing trip, but the $18 sweater is made of acrylic, a fabric that Stephen sometimes finds irritating. Further, because the sweater has a pattern, it might not fit well into his wardrobe.

On the grounds of fabric content alone, Stephen would like to purchase the cotton sweater, because cotton is very comfortable. The cotton sweater, however, is the most expensive, and white is not Stephen's favorite color.

Finally, the wool sweater is a somewhat drab gray, but the wool would certainly be warm. The price of the wool sweater is less than that of the cotton sweater, though it is more than that of the acrylic sweater.

After trying on all three sweaters and viewing them in the mirror, Stephen decides that before he makes a purchase he will investigate the possibility of buying a lightweight jacket.

Now we analyze the decision or situation.

By decision or situation, we mean Stephen's thinking about which sweater to buy. Notice that the discussion never culminates in a final choice, and this is typical of the GMAT format. You are asked to evaluate the process—not to make a final choice.

With regard to the process of Stephen's thinking, we first note that Stephen finds himself in a situation that has a definite structure; he has only $100 to spend, but he needs a sweater because the weather has turned cool. Second, Stephen has certain goals that he wants to achieve: he wants to have enough money left after his purchase to enjoy the rest of the trip. Third, the options (the different sweaters) are different from each other in important ways; each sweater has a different price tag.

The following table summarizes this analysis:

Structural Features	Goals to be Achieved	Relevant Differences in Options
Because of weather Stephen must buy a sweater. He has three options.	Stephen wants to pick the best sweater for him.	Each option is more or less desirable compared to other options.
He has $100 in traveler's checks.	He wants to avoid spending too much.	A sweater costs more or less than the others.
He has wardrobe requirements and style preferences.	He wants a sweater that will fit his wardrobe and look nice.	A sweater looks better or worse on Stephen, including matching his other clothes.
He has fabric preferences.	He wants a fabric that will be serviceable and comfortable.	A sweater has a fabric that is better or worse for Stephen.

Organizing the aspects of the decision in this way clarifies several further points about the logic of a decisional situation. First, the structural features (first category) could be classified into three types: those creating the need for a decision, those limiting the courses of action, and those establishing what differences are relevant. It is the change in weather and Stephen's lack of proper clothing that create the very need for a decision. Stephen's size and the stock available in the store dictate that only three sweaters (of all the sweaters in the world) are available options. Then, Stephen's relative lack of money establishes that the difference in price is a relevant difference. Stephen's wardrobe requirements and style preferences establish that Stephen should compare the color of each sweater against the others. Finally, the fact that Stephen has fabric preferences means that the difference in fabric content will be relevant.

With regard to Stephen's goals, we note two things. First, there is a close logical connection between some of the goals and some of the structural features; Stephen *has only* $100 and he *wants to save* as much of that as possible. These two attitudes or judgments are related to each other, but they are not the same. On the one hand, if Stephen had unlimited funds, then we would not count among his goals saving money. On the other hand, that Stephen *wants* to save money is not the same thing as his *need* to save money. Second, Stephen's wants are incompatible—his top choice in terms of fabric (the cotton sweater) is his bottom choice in terms of price. In other words, any choice will be a compromise, and is this not what often makes decisions difficult?

In relation to the relevant differences, we note that a difference, to be a difference that makes a difference, must be related to some goal (and therefore indirectly to some structural feature). For example, if Stephen did have unlimited funds and not just $100, so that he did not consider saving money something to be achieved, the difference in price among the sweaters would just not be relevant. Similarly, someone else might see differences that Stephen has chosen to disregard; for example, whether a sweater is imported or not. Whereas some buyers might wish to purchase a sweater made by American labor and would consider an imported or domestic distinction to be important, Stephen apparently does not have such a goal and the question does not arise.

> **97** Learn to understand a decision in terms of the structure of the situation, the goals to be achieved, and the relevant differences between options.

You can check your understanding of these points and sharpen your ability to apply them to new situations by using them to analyze ordinary decisions that you make every day. For example, you are sitting in a restaurant and must order a meal. What features structure the situation? (The available menu items; spending limit; time allowed for lunch; being on a diet.) What are the goals you would like to achieve? (Save money; eat quickly to get back to your desk; lose some weight; enjoy the meal.) What are the differences between the options? (Taste; price; time needed for each meal; calories contained in the meals.) Of course, we do not all think alike. For some of us calories will not be important, for others they will be of real concern. Similarly, for some, money will not be a relevant consideration, yet for others it will be. But no matter what specific concerns you have, you should still be able to determine the logical role they play.

UNDERSTANDING THE DIRECTIONS

Let us now introduce sketches of five decisions. These are summaries of situations that the GMAT would describe in detail using 900 or 1,000 words. We will use the sketches to illustrate each answer choice category.

Five Sketches of Decisional Problems

Case 1

Company *XYZ* has a contract to deliver 5,000 widgets by August 1, but on July 1 the widget-making machine breaks down. Smith, President of *XYZ*, determines that five companies, *E, F, G, H*, and *I*, have widget-making machines for sale. Since Smith has a deadline to meet, and since Smith wants to make a profit, she studies each machine in terms of its cost, the date it could be delivered, and its reliability.

Case 2

Company *PQR*, a furniture manufacturer, is doing well and has a cash surplus, but the Board of Directors is worried that the future is not so rosy. They decide to diversify by buying a smaller company: a widget factory, a brewery, or a baseball team. The Board studies each company's profitability and the potential for expansion into each company's market.

Case 3

Jones owns a clothing store, but his lease will expire in two months. Since the landlord refuses to renew, Jones must relocate to one of four properties: 19 Elm Street, 23 Main Street, 26 Harvey Square, or 255 Boulevard. Jones wants to find a long-term lease, with a low monthly rental, at a location that will be good for business, so he examines each possible store by reading the lease offered and by studying the conditions that might affect business.

Case 4

A baseball club is experiencing serious financial problems, and in an effort to increase ticket sales the owner is trying to decide whether to hire new players with national reputations, cut ticket prices, intensify giveaways at the stadium, or some combination of the three. The owner wants a winning team, so he is concerned about the quality of his players, and the owner wants a financially viable operation, so he is worried about costs and about risk.

Case 5

A small college has built a new campus, leaving its old building vacant. It must dispose of the old building by selling it. The administration is considering selling the building to a developer who will convert it to condominiums; selling it to a different developer who will tear it down and put up a high-rise office building; or selling it to a restaurateur. The administration of the college considers the pros and cons of each proposed use of the building, including the effect on the neighborhood, and the financial terms of each offer.

Key 98 summarizes the relationship between the categories we used to analyze Stephen's decision about which sweater to buy and the answer choices used by the GMAT:

Key 98
Structure of the situation = (D)
Goals to be achieved = (A)
Differences used to compare options = (B) or (C)
Other = (E)

Now we will study each answer choice.

According to the directions for this section, you answer "(D) if the item is a *Major Assumption* in making the decision; that is, a supposition or projection made by the decision maker before weighing the variables." Several points of clarification are in order. First:

Key 99 For (D)s, ignore the word "major."

The directions for the exam are set up so that an item is either an (A), (B), (C), or (D) or else it is irrelevant. There is no middle category "Minor Assumption" between answer choice (D) and answer choice (E) (unimportant issue). Logically, such a category is possible, but the test writers never use it. So the word "major," as applied to choice (D), is simply superfluous. Any item that is a structural feature of a situation must be classified as a (D)—without regard to its relative importance. The GMAT does not divide (D)s into these subcategories, but (D)s will be easier to identify if you keep in mind the three different types of structural features. We will illustrate each type with the preceding case sketches.

Key 100 Mark an item as (D) if it creates the need for the decision.

Case 1

The breakdown of the machine and the impossibility of repairing it in time creates the need for deciding which replacement to buy, so the impossibility of completing the production without finding a replacement would be classified as a (D).

Case 2

The possibility that the company might not do well in the future prompts the directors to consider diversifying, so the possibility of future problems, creating the need for the decision, would be classified as a (D).

Case 3

Because the lease is expiring, Jones must find a new location for his store. The expiration of the lease, the cause of Jones's problem, would be classified as a (D).

Case 4

The poor financial picture of the club makes it necessary for the owner to take some action, so the financial crisis would be classified as a (D).

Case 5

The college owns a building that it must dispose of, and this prompts the administration to entertain offers for the building. The vacancy of the building prompts the decision and would be classified as a (D).

Therefore, you mark as a (D) any item that prompts the decision maker to undertake to make the decision in the first place. Furthermore:

> **101** Mark an item as (D) if it helps to define the availability and feasibility of the options.

Case 1

Since five companies, E, F, G, H, and I have available replacement machines, Smith has five options—no more, no less. This is clearly something that structures Smith's decision, so the availability of five machines would be classified as a (D).

Case 2

The Board knows of three companies for sale that would be suitable for their needs. The availability of those three companies for sale would be classified as a (D).

Case 3

Jones knows of four available locations. Those are the only options he has to consider, so the availability of leases at those locations structures Jones's decision and is a (D). If the 19 Elm Street location were already rented, it would not be a live option. So its availability, and similarly, the availability of the other locations, is a (D).

Case 4

In this case the options are a bit more abstract, than the three preceding cases because they are not represented by concrete objects such as machines or stores. Still, the feasibility of hiring a new player, or of cutting prices, or of intensifying giveaways is needed to set up the option; that is, if there were no other players available for hire for whatever reason, then the option of hiring new players would not be open. So the feasibility of taking one of the actions described would be classified as a (D).

Case 5

The administration of the college has received three bids on its building, and these are the only options open to the college. So the receipt of three bids and no more nor any less constitutes a (D).

> **102** Mark an item as (D) if it establishes what differences between options are relevant.

It is important to keep in mind that options (e.g., sweaters) may vary in many ways: color, fabric, price, maker, style, or cleaning care required. Not all of these are necessarily important. To a decision maker with unlimited funds, price will be irrelevant. The relevance of some difference depends upon a corresponding structural feature of the decision that commits the decision maker to regard that difference as important:

Case 1

Smith faces a deadline, and this tells her that any difference between machines in terms of delivery or reliability that would affect her ability to meet the deadline is relevant. If Smith had no deadline, then she would not care when she finished the work, and she would not study the machines in terms of when they could be delivered or when they would finish the work. Similarly, Smith is in business to make a profit, so she operates within cost guidelines. Consequently, she compares the cost of each machine. Thus, the deadline for finishing the work makes relevant the differences in delivery dates and the reliability, and so is a (D). Further, the necessity for keeping costs low enough to make a profit requires Smith to pay attention to price. This too is a (D).

Case 2

Apparently the Board of Directors of *PQR* is concerned with one thing only: money. The need to keep doing good business establishes the relevance of the only two differences between options, the profitability and the potential for expansion. Thus, the importance of making a profit and the importance of expanding are (D)s.

Case 3

In this case, there are three relevant differences between options: monthly rental, length of lease, and market. The amount of rent Jones would have to pay at each location is made important because Jones realizes he cannot stay in business if his rent is too high, so the need to keep the rent low is a (D). Similarly, Jones thinks a long-term lease is important, otherwise he would not consider the length of lease offered at each location. Also Jones realizes that a store without customers is no good at all, so he considers the market conditions at each location. Therefore, the relationship between the neighborhood surrounding the store and the potential for its success is a (D).

Case 4

Because the team must make money, the owner compares the possible courses of action in terms of their ability to solve the financial problem and in terms of the risk they present. So the need to maintain the profitability of the team is a (D). To prove this, make the opposite assumption about the structure of the decision. If the owner regarded the team as a hobby and did not regard making a profit as important at all, the owner would not worry about the financial consequences of the decision. Also the importance of fielding a winning team is a (D), for if the owner did not care about the success of the team, then he would not evaluate his options in terms of whether they would contribute to the team's success.

Case 5

The college has a need for money, for the administration considers the financial terms of each offer. Therefore the college's need for money is a (D).

> **103** Do not confuse the structural features of the situation with the goals or the differences between options.

It is very important that you do not confuse the structural features of the situation with the other elements we have identified. There is a subtle but critical distinction between the *need to keep the rent low* (structural feature); *finding a location with a low rent* (goal to be achieved); and *the monthly rental charged at each location* (an important difference between each location). Similarly, *the deadline that Smith must meet* (structural feature) is not the same thing as *finding a machine* to meet that deadline (goal to be achieved); and those are both different from the different *dates by which each machine could be delivered* (the difference by which options can be compared to each other).

There is a third point to be made about (D)s:

> **104** Be alert for structural features that the decision maker must be aware of and is relying on but does not explicitly mention. These too are (D)s.

Try describing a decisional situation to a friend. Likely, there are some important structural features that you will not explicitly touch on but which you presuppose your friend will understand to be operative in your analysis. For example, if you say "I looked at the menu and the prices were fairly expensive," your friend will appreciate, without further elaboration, that you, like most of us, operate under some financial constraint. This financial constraint functions as a (D) in your decision. In the cases sketched previously, we also find such implicit (D)s:

Case 1

Smith apparently presupposes that each machine she is considering can produce widgets of the quality that she needs. The proof of this is easy: suppose that the machine offered by Company G produced widgets of a quality below that required by Smith, would she even be considering the price or delivery date of that machine? No! So Smith must be aware of the quality of work that would be done by the machines and implicitly accept it. Thus the ability of each machine to do an acceptable job would be a (D).

Case 2

We did not explicitly mention that the owners of the smaller companies were willing to sell to *PQR*. Yet, the Board of *PQR* must be aware of their willingness to sell, otherwise the Board would not entertain the widget factory, the brewery, and the baseball team as viable options. So, the willingness of owners to sell would be a (D).

Case 3

One implicit (D) in this case is the suitability of each store to Jones's needs. There is no discussion of the size of the stores. Apparently, Jones is aware that each store is acceptable in terms of size, so each store is a live option. Consider what the situation would be if Jones determined that neither the 19 Elm Street location nor the 23 Main Street location was sufficiently large for his purposes. In that case, only two options would remain. So the acceptability of each store in terms of its size would be a (D).

Case 4

The owner of the club must believe that some action on his part does have the possibility of solving the crisis he faces. After all, if the club were doomed to financial failure no matter what, he would not be considering action. So the possibility of solving the crisis, assuming a suitable remedy can be found, is a (D). Further, the case sketch does not explicitly state that there are players with a national reputation who are available for hire and who would be willing to play for the owner, yet we know that the owner must believe this, for he considers the possibility of hiring such players a live option. So the availability of players with national reputations and the willingness of such players to play for the owner must be (D)s.

Case 5

The administration of the college wants to dispose of its building, yet the administration apparently feels it has some continuing obligation to the community. Otherwise, the administration would simply accept the best financial offer. Because the administration does consider the pros and cons of each proposed use of the building, we can infer that the administration is aware of an obligation to the community. So the requirement that the college respect the community's integrity is a (D).

These are not the only implicit (D)s in our sketches, but they do illustrate the point.

Next, we consider category (A). Mark "(A) if the item is a *Major Objective* in making the decision; that is, one of the outcomes or results sought by the decision maker."

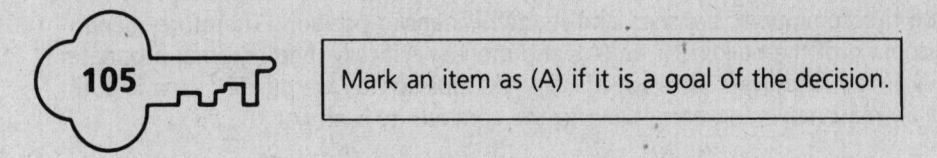

105 Mark an item as (A) if it is a goal of the decision.

And this is true without regard to the seeming importance of the goal:

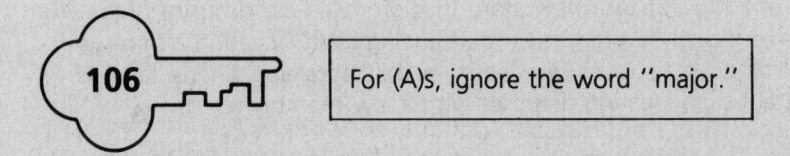

106 For (A)s, ignore the word "major."

The analysis of (D)s applies here as well. There is no "Minor Objective" category, so the word "Major" is simply superfluous. Anything that is a goal of the decision is to be classified as an (A):

Case 1

Smith wants to meet her deadline, and she wants to make a profit, so finding a machine to meet the deadline and keeping the cost of doing so to a minimum are both (A)s.

Case 2

The Board wants to ensure the financial security of the company. To do this, the Board hopes to buy a company that is profitable and that has the potential for expansion. So diversifying by buying another company, guaranteeing the financial viability of *PQR*, buying a profitable company, and acquiring a company with potential for expansion are all (A)s.

Case 3

Jones wants to find a new store, and he judges the desirability of each location by the rent he would have to pay, length of the lease offered, and the business conditions surrounding each location. So finding a new store location is an (A), and we would also classify finding a store with a low rent, finding a store with a long lease, and finding a store in a good business area as (A)s.

Case 4

The owner wants to win baseball games and he wants to stay in business, so a successful team and a financially viable operation are (A)s.

Case 5

The college wants to dispose of its old building, and it wants to do so while respecting the community's wishes and its own financial position. Therefore, generally, disposing of the building is an (A), and more specifically, finding an appropriate buyer is an (A), and even more specifically, a disposition of the building that is both financially reasonable and acceptable to the community is an (A).

You should observe that we have classified items as (A)s, because they function as goals of a decision—without regard to the relative weight accorded them. Thus, in Case 3, finding a new location, obtaining a long lease, locating premises with a low monthly rental, and moving to a new store that promises good business conditions are all (A)s, even though it might seem that finding a new location is in some sense more "major" than obtaining a long lease, or that obtaining a long lease is somehow less important than locating premises with a low monthly rental.

107 | The typical GMAT decision has several "major objectives" (A).

Next, we take up the categories of major and minor factor. The instructions say to mark an item as:

> (B) if the item is a *Major Factor* in making the decision; that is, a consideration, explicitly mentioned in the passage, that is basic in determining the decision.

and

> (C) if the item is a *Minor Factor* in making the decision; that is, a secondary consideration that affects the criteria tangentially, relating to a major factor rather than to an objective.

As we see from the table of correspondences in Key 98, the factors are the differences between options; that is, the aspects of the options that make an option better or worse than another option. Setting aside the question of distinguishing (B)s from (C)s, we isolate the "factors" in the five sketches:

Case 1

Smith compares one machine to another in terms of the date it would be delivered, in terms of the purchase price, and in terms of reliability. So the date each machine would be delivered, the price or cost of each machine, and the reliability of each machine are the "factors" in Smith's decision.

Case 2

The Board studies two features of each company they are considering for purchase: the profitability of the company and the company's potential for expansion. So profitability and potential for expansion are the "factors" considered by the Board.

Case 3

Jones compares the new locations along three lines: the monthly rental, the length of lease offered, and the business conditions. So the monthly rent of each store, the length of lease offered at each location, and the business conditions at each store are the "factors" in Jones's decision.

Case 4

What are the questions the owner asks in deciding on the best option? The owner asks "Will this solve the financial crisis?" and "Will this help to make a winning team?" So the ability of each proposal to solve the financial crisis and the contribution each proposal would make to the success of the team are the "factors" in the owner's decision.

Case 5

The administration debates the pros and cons of each of the proposed dispositions: this is a better financial offer than that; this disposition would result in the destruction of the building. The financial terms of the various offers and the use intended by each of the bidders are the "factors" in the college's decision. So:

> **Key 108:** Mark an item as either (B) or (C) if it is one of the differences between options that the decision maker uses to compare one option to another.

Of course, this does not yet distinguish the (B)s from the (C)s, and for that we need another key:

> **Key 109:** To distinguish (B)s from (C)s, use the rule of subordination: if a factor is *logically* subordinate to some other factor it is a (C); if it is not, it is a (B).

The rule of subordination is a principle of organization. Once you have determined that an item is a "factor," you then ascertain whether that item is logically subordinate to some other item. If it is subordinate, mark it a (C); otherwise, the item is a (B).

The application of the rule is easily demonstrated in the following familiar situation:

> Peter goes to his favorite restaurant for lunch. He has $20 in his pocket, and he is watching his weight. This is the menu.

MENU

Spinach Salad	$5.95
Burger with Fries	$4.50
Fried Chicken with Mashed Potatoes	$7.95
Sauteed Liver and Onions	$6.25
Omelette	$4.95

Peter immediately eliminates the liver from consideration on the grounds that he dislikes liver. Further, Peter will not consider the omelette since he had eggs for breakfast.

Peter considers first the cost of each of the remaining meals, including the 5 percent sales tax and a 15 percent tip:

Cost Calculation

	Spinach Salad	Burger	Fried Chicken
Menu Price	$5.95	$4.50	$7.95
Tax	.30	.23	.40
Tip	.90	.68	1.20
Total	$7.15	$5.41	$9.55

Next Peter considers the nutritional content of each meal. The spinach salad is low in calories and very high in iron and other minerals and vitamins. The burger has more calories than the spinach salad but fewer than the fried chicken, but the burger is red meat and the fried chicken is poultry, and Peter is concerned about eating too much fatty red meat. The chicken is very high in calories because it is fried in oil.

Finally, Peter considers the taste of each meal. Though the spinach salad is very nutritious, its taste is not very interesting when compared to a burger or fried chicken. The fried chicken is one of Peter's favorites, and he would enjoy it even more than the burger.

Before ordering, Peter decided to ask the waiter whether there were any specials of the day not listed on the menu.

How does Peter compare his options? He compares the various meals in terms of cost, in terms of food content, and in terms of taste. These are the "factors" of the decision. Here, however, we have developed the discussion of the "factors" in greater detail than we did before in our five sketches. In discussing cost, for example, we break down the cost according to the menu price, the tax, and the tip, and each of these must in turn be considered a factor. But should we call the tax on a meal a (B) or a (C)? What about the total cost of the meals? (B) or (C)?

To answer these questions we have recourse to the rule of subordination. The tax on the meals should be labeled a (C), because the tax is logically subordinate to the total cost of the meals, that is, tax is only one component of the cost calculation. The total cost, however, should be called a (B) because it is not logically subordinate to any further consideration—it is the bottom line, so to speak.

Similarly, the nutritional content of each meal is a "factor" that is developed in some detail. Peter thinks about the vitamins and minerals in the food, and he thinks about the number of calories in the various dishes. So the nutritional content of each meal, the various vitamins and minerals in the food, and the number of calories in each dish are all "factors." Using the rule of subordination, we would classify the various vitamins and minerals in the food as a (C), because this is just one aspect of the nutritional content; that is, vitamins and minerals are logically subordinated by Peter to the more general idea of nutritional content. Similarly, we would classify the calorie content in the various meals as a (C), for the number of calories is an aspect of nutritional content. Nutritional content, however, is not subordinated to anything else, so it would be classified as a (B).

Finally, Peter considers the taste of each meal, and this too is a "factor." The aspect of taste is not developed in as much detail as the other factors, so how should we classify the taste of each meal? Since it is not logically subordinate to some other consideration, the taste of the meals is a (B). The fact that there is nothing logically subordinate to taste is irrelevant. The rule of subordination requires that you ask whether the item, as a factor, is logically subordinated by the decision maker to some other factor. Since the taste of the meal is not subordinated, it must be a (B).

We move quickly to answer the possible objection that the rule of subordination does not respect the wording of the directions "Major" and "Minor." Those who voice this objection will attempt to subordinate nutritional content to taste, or cost to nutritional content by arguing that one or the other must be more important. This is an error. There is no way to determine which of the three "factors" is the most important to Peter, so it would be futile to attempt to distinguish (B)s from (C)s on that ground. Rather, the terms "major" and "minor" are intended to have a *logical* significance. In a sense, the total cost of the meal is "more important" than any of the components, menu price, tax, or tip. And it does seem that the number of calories in a meal is somehow "less important" a consideration than the overall nutritional content which includes, as it does, the calorie consideration. So the (B)–(C) distinction applies within a set of differences, not across the sets of differences:

> **110** The rule of subordination applies within groups of differences, not across groups. As a result, a typical GMAT passage will have two or more (B)s.

In Peter's decision, there are three sets of differences: cost, nutritional content, and taste. The rule applies within each set to establish that the total cost of the meal is a (B), the nutritional content of a meal is a (B), and the taste of a meal is a (B). Within each category, every detail is a (C). The rule, however, is not to be used to compare taste with cost or nutritional content with taste.

The final category, (E), is reserved for those items that play no active role in the decision:

> Mark (E) if the item is an *Unimportant Issue* in making the decision; that is, a factor that is insignificant or not immediately relevant to the situation.

Again, the status of an item as irrelevant is determined by its logical role in the decisional analysis:

> **111** Mark as (E) any item that belongs entirely in the past.

Most GMAT decisions begin with some background information. If Case 5 were an actual GMAT problem, the first paragraph or two would most likely provide some background information:

> Small College was founded in 1927 by Dr. George Barnes, to provide a liberal arts education for the children of nearby farms. Dr. Barnes headed the

college for nearly 50 years, until his death in 1975. At that time, Professor Eleanor Newsome, head of the History Department, was elected President of the college. Professor Newsome realized that the college had outgrown its one four-story building, so she initiated an aggressive fund-raising campaign to build a new campus. In 1982, the new campus was completed, at a cost of $17 million. In early 1983 all college operations were moved to the new campus leaving the old building vacant. Professor Newsome feared that the vacant building would rapidly deteriorate and called a meeting of the Building Committee to discuss the sale of the building.

At this point would begin a discussion of the available options and the pros and cons of each.

The information that precedes the statement of the decision to be made is interesting and provides the reader with a point of reference, but it is not logically necessary to the decision. Therefore, the length of time that Dr. Barnes was head of the college, why the college grew, why the decision was made to build a new campus, the manner in which Professor Newsome raised the money for the new campus, and all similar items would be classified as (E)s.

112 Mark as (E) any item indicated by the decision maker to be insignificant.

Sometimes an idea will specifically be labeled as unimportant. For example, it might be pointed out that one machine has a larger cab than any of the other machines being considered for purchase; but if the passage then goes on to state that all machines have cabs of adequate size and that this extra room serves no useful function, then the extra room provided in the cab of that machine must be considered an (E). Or it might have been pointed out that one of the locations in Case 3 required repainting. If the case then went on to say that the landlord had agreed to bear that cost, then the cost of repainting the premises would be considered an (E).

113 Mark as (E) any item that is collateral to the decision.

Finally, there are some items which seem to be related to the general problem situation but which are collateral to the real decision. It might be mentioned in passing, for example, that Smith (Case 1) makes not only widgets but paper clips. Since the decision focuses on the widget-making machine, improving the productive capability of the paper-clip-producing machine would be considered an (E).

RECOGNIZING THE SIGNIFICANCE OF AN ITEM'S PHRASING

The directions for this section require that you classify "items" according to the categories we have studied. These "items" are sentence fragments intended to refer to some aspect of the decision. This means the questions in this section are not really questions at all. They are not complete sentences with subject and verb; they are only sentence fragments:

> **114** Learn to recognize the significance of an item's phrasing.

To pursue this line of thought, we need a situation sufficiently rich in detail to support many fragments. Familiarize yourself with the following situation:

Ashley Andersen will graduate from the State University at the end of the spring semester with a Master's in Business Administration. Her education was financed in part by income she received from a trust fund established for that purpose by her grandmother. Now that Ashley's education is complete, she will receive the body of the trust fund, approximately $175,000. Ashley has decided to invest the money in a business that she can own and manage herself. In this way, she will be able to support herself while putting her education to practical use. After examining several business opportunities, Ashley decided to purchase a franchise for the operation of a restaurant. Her local bank has promised to lend her up to $50,000, if she decides she needs it.

The State University is located in Sparta, and it is there Ashley plans to open her restaurant. The town has a population of 175,000, but that number swells to 225,000 when school is in session. There are already a number of restaurants and cafes scattered throughout the area, but the students tend not to patronize these establishments because they do not wish to associate closely with the town's residents. Ashley believes that a fast-food restaurant with an attractive new physical plant would attract a substantial number of students and would also be patronized by the town's population. Ashley has procured from several franchising organizations copies of the prospectuses they are required by law to file with the U.S. Securities and Exchange Commission (SEC) when they offer a restaurant franchise for sale. She has finally narrowed her choice to three: McCarthy's Burgers, Royal Pizza, and Carolina Chicken.

Ashley studied each prospectus to determine what initial capital would be required and how profitable she could expect the franchise to be. Ashley also wanted to make sure she would have an opportunity to apply her managerial skills in operating the franchise.

The McCarthy's Burgers prospectus contained the following information:

McCarthy's began 15 years ago in Southern California as Bingo Burgers. It was started by a retired Army officer who expanded the business until it included a small chain of three restaurants. At that time, he sold the operation to a group of investors who began to franchise it. There are now over 2,500 McCarthy's stores across the nation. McCarthy's specializes in providing inexpensive, fast food such as hamburgers and french fries. The typical McCarthy's meal, consisting of a hamburger, french fries, and a soft drink, costs about $2.75

McCarthy's carries on an extensive nationwide advertising campaign financed and paid for entirely by the national office. This advertising campaign includes massive print and television advertising, and the national office frequently sponsors special sales promotions such as holiday gift certificates.

The supplies used by a McCarthy's restaurant, including all food and paper products, must be purchased from the regional commissary. In this way, the national office is able to ensure that quality does not vary from store to store. This uniformity of quality redounds to the benefit of every McCarthy's franchise.

All new McCarthy's franchise owners are required to attend a three-week training program. In this program, franchisees are instructed in techniques of food processing, personnel management, accounting, and other activities essential to operating a profitable store.

The franchise fee for a McCarthy's restaurant is $100,000, and in addition the franchisee must pay a royalty equal to 5 percent of the gross receipts taken in by the store each month.

The Royal Pizza prospectus contained the following information:

Royal Pizza is not an ordinary fast-food franchise. The food served at a Royal Pizza restaurant is made to order. Customers can choose from among 12 different ingredients and three different sizes of pizzas. Additionally, Royal Pizza encourages franchise holders to apply for a license to sell beer and wine for these beverages go naturally with pizza and are high-profit items. A typical meal for two at Royal Pizza consists of a medium or large pizza and soft drinks at a price of $7.50, or $11.25 if wine or beer is substituted for soft drinks.

Royal Pizza has now been a franchise operation for 4 years and there are 23 Royal Pizza franchise stores in this region. Recently, the head office has undertaken to assist franchise holders in promoting their restaurants. The head office is now placing weekly advertisements in the Sunday editions of the three largest regional papers. Additionally, the head office subsidizes "coupon" promotional campaigns when undertaken by individual franchisees.

A representative from the head office will spend one or two days at a new store when it opens to make sure that the start-up goes smoothly. Then, every month, someone from the head office will visit each store and answer questions about restaurant management. Additionally, the head office is always reachable by telephone should a franchisee need further advice.

Furthermore, Royal Pizza franchise contracts contain no commissary provision. You are free to purchase your supplies from whomever you choose and at whatever price you are able to negotiate. In this way, you are not bound to order products you do not need, and you do not have to pay a price you do not like.

The initial franchise fee for a Royal Pizza restaurant is only $25,000. Should a franchise elect to procure a license to sell beer and wine, it is expected that another $15,000 will be required for the state licensing fees. All Royal Pizza restaurants pay 2½ percent of gross receipts to the head office on a monthly basis.

The Carolina Chicken prospectus provided the following information:

Carolina Chicken, Inc., is a rapidly expanding chain of restaurants specializing in fried chicken. There are currently 175 Carolina Chicken stores across the country, concentrated primarily in the Midwest. It is the goal of management to have over 750 such stores in operation within 5 years. This will allow headquarters to do even more regional and national advertising. You have probably seen television spots for Carolina Chicken on your local station.

Fried chicken is now a viable alternative to the typical hamburger-oriented fast-food restaurant. A typical Carolina Chicken meal consists of two or three pieces of fried chicken, a biscuit, and coleslaw or french fries served in an attractive red, white, and blue box. The cost of a typical meal is only $2.65, making it an attractive alternative for low-budget eaters.

The Carolina Chicken franchise requires an initial franchise fee of $40,000, and each franchise pays a monthly royalty of 4 percent of gross receipts. Before a franchise begins operation of a Carolina Chicken franchise, he or she visits corporate headquarters for a three-day indoctrination program. In this program, top-level management discuss all aspects of managing a Carolina Chicken restaurant. When a franchisee is ready to begin operation, a corporate vice president will visit the store to help with hiring and ordering supplies from the commissary.

Having familiarized herself with the offering prospectus of each chain, Ashley considered each franchisee in greater detail. She was favorably impressed by the extensive training offered by McCarthy's, for although she had good theoretical training, she had never before been involved in the day-to-day operation of a restaurant. On the other hand, Ashley considered that the strict supervision exercised by McCarthy's management might prevent her from implementing her own ideas. There would be no opportunity to vary the menu or experiment with new marketing ideas. At the other extreme was the Royal Pizza franchise. It offered very little in the way of restaurant training, but then again it seemed to encourage individual entrepreneurs. Ashley liked the idea of selling wine and beer and catering to the student trade, perhaps even offering live entertainment such as piano or folk music.

Ashley was also concerned with the profit potential of each restaurant. The royalty required for the McCarthy's restaurant was very high and that would cut into profits, but she also had to consider that the national office did considerably more advertising for its franchises than the other chains. That advertising would probably result in more customers for Ashley's restaurant. Additionally, Ashley knew that a franchisor usually made a profit on items sold through its commissary. While a commissary provision does guarantee nationwide quality, it also means a lower profit margin for the individual franchisee. The Royal Pizza franchise had the merit of encouraging sales of beer and wine, high-profit beverages, and the sale of alcohol was strictly prohibited by the franchise agreements of McCarthy's and Carolina Chicken. In an attempt to get a rough idea of the annual gross receipts she could expect from each franchise, Ashley used the average meal price mentioned in each prospectus and made a rough estimate of the number of customers she might attract:

	Price of Average Meal	Expected Number of Patrons (Daily; 7-day week)	Gross Receipts (Annualized)
McCarthy's	$ 2.75	1,2000	$1.2 million
Royal Pizza	$11.25	300	$1.23 million
Carolina Chicken	$ 2.65	1,000	$ .97 million

Finally, Ashley realized that her initial investment would have to cover not only the franchise fee charged by each chain; there were expenses for land, physical plant, and furnishings which she summarized:

START-UP COSTS

	McCarthy's	Carolina Chicken	Royal Pizza
Franchise Fee	$100,000	$ 40,000	$ 25,000
Land	10,000	10,000	10,000
Building	70,000	65,000	80,000
Landscaping	5,000	3,000	5,500
Furnishings	18,000	17,000	19,000
Kitchen Equip.	16,000	19,000	28,000
Addition fees	———	———	15,000*
Totals	$219,000	$154,000	$182,500

*License for beer and wine

Some Possible (A)s

Operating a successful fast-food restaurant that will provide an opportunity to exercise business skills.
A profitable franchised fast-food restaurant operation.
A low initial start-up cost.
Flexibility in implementing individual decisions on matters of restaurant policy.
Applying skills learned in school in a practical situation.

Some Possible (B)s

Initial investment required to start up a fast-food franchise.
Profit that would be realized under each one of the arrangements being considered.
Amount of leeway offered to owner by each franchise to implement individual management ideas.

Some Possible (C)s

Cost of kitchen equipment for each of the restaurants being studied.
Additional fee required for a liquor license.
Number of customers that would be likely to patronize each of the restaurants.
Stricter control over operations exercised by McCarthy's Burgers.
Opportunity provided by Royal Pizza to introduce live entertainment.

Some Possible (D)s

Bank credit of up to $50,000 for start-up costs.
Unsatisfactoriness of any business not allowing sufficient opportunity for managerial discretion.
Distribution of the corpus of the educational trust fund upon graduation.
Ashley's ability to successfully manage a franchise restaurant.

Some Possible (E)s

Government laws regulating the content of prospectuses for the sale of franchises.
Labor costs incurred in running a typical franchise restaurant.
Existence of other restaurants and cafes in the Sparta area.
Learning further theoretical business skills.

Of course, the list is not exhaustive. Other fragments could be added; and there are still other ways of writing the items that are included in the list. For this reason it is not possible to provide a list of typical phrasings; instead we recommend you use the sentence completion method. Place the fragment in the question into a sentence that describes the function you think the fragment refers to, and if the result is a complete sentence that makes sense, then you have found the correct choice:

> **115** A sentence completion test for (A)s: "———" is one of the outcomes or results sought by the decision maker.

In the list of possible (A)s, we have "Applying skills learned in school in a practical situation." When tested by the sentence completion method, the fragment yields:

> Applying skills learned in school in a practical situation is one of the outcomes or results sought by Ashley.

This sentence is an accurate description of Ashley's thinking, so the fragment is indeed an (A). If, however, we take a fragment from a different category, say a (C), the sentence will not be a correct description of Ashley's thinking:

Stricter control over operations exercised by McCarthy's Burgers is one of the outcomes or results sought by Ashley.

Since this statement is inaccurate, the fragment cannot be an (A).

Sometimes the wording of a fragment will be strange or awkward, and the result of a test using the form just provided may not be clear. If the result using Key 115 is ambiguous, use the alternative test for (A)s:

> **116** An alternative sentence completion test for (A)s: The decision maker would like "———."

The alternative test is more suitable for fragments such as "a low initial start-up cost," because the result of the first sentence completion may sound strange to the ear:

A low initial start-up cost is one of the outcomes or results sought by Ashley.

Strictly speaking, this is an accurate description of the decision, but the awkwardness of the sentence may obscure the result of the test. The alternative sentence, when completed, reads more smoothly:

Ashley would like a low initial start-up cost.

There is one danger to be alert for when using the sentence completion method for (A)s:

> **117** Watch out for fragments that make a semantically correct statement substantively incorrect.

Consider the following two uses of the sentence completion method:

Ashley would like bank credit of up to $50,000 for start-up costs.

Profit that would be realized under each one of the arrangements being considered is one of the outcomes or results sought by Ashley.

On first reading, these assertions seem plausible, but closer attention to the substance of the assertions shows them to be incorrect. First, Ashley already has the bank credit; the credit is not something she can obtain by making a decision on which franchise to purchase. The first statement is not an accurate description of Ashley's thinking and the second statement is also incorrect. Though Ashley wants to make a profit, she cannot hope to realize the profit that could be made under *each one* of the franchises. She can only purchase one franchise, not all three.

The item "bank credit" is a (D), and this can be demonstrated by using a sentence completion test designed for (D)s:

> **118**
>
> A sentence completion test for (D)s:
> "_____" helps to structure the decision by (1) creating the need to make the decision; (2) establishing the feasibility of the options; or (3) determining the criteria by which the options are to be compared.

Substituting the fragment in question into the sentence, the result is this:

> Bank credit of up to $50,000 for start-up costs helps to structure the decision by determining the feasibility of the options.

This is an accurate statement, for without the bank credit, Ashley would not have sufficient funds to open a restaurant.

A similar test is available for (B)s and (C)s, but we must distinguish between two types of wording. Some factors specifically mention one of the options by name; others refer generally to a group of options:

> Profit that would be realized under each one of the arrangements being considered
> Cost of kitchen equipment for each of the restaurants being studied
> Stricter control over operations exercised by McCarthy's Burgers

The first two fragments refer generally to the entire set of options. The third fragment refers only to the McCarthy's franchise. This slight variation makes it necessary to have two tests for (B)s and (C)s:

> **119**
>
> Sentence completion test for (B)s and (C)s: When the fragment refers to an option by name: "_____" is considered by the decision maker to be an advantage (disadvantage) of the option. When the fragment refers generally to a group of options: The decision maker compares these options to one another in terms of the "_____."

For the third fragment above, the sentence completion test works as follows:

> Stricter control over operations exercised by McCarthy's Burgers is considered by Ashley to be a disadvantage of the McCarthy's franchise.

This is an accurate description of the situation, so the fragment is either a (C) or a (B). Using the rule of subordination, we recognize the fragment as a (C), since McCarthy's policies are just one aspect of the more extensive discussion of the flexibility Ashley would have. For the other two fragments we use the sentence designed for general wording:

> Ashley compares the options to one another in terms of the profit that would be realized under each one of the arrangements being considered.
>
> Ashley compares the options to one another in terms of the cost of kitchen equipment for each of the restaurants being studied.

Both sentences are accurate, if slightly awkward. The awkwardness can be eliminated by trimming the redundancy created by using the full wording of the fragment:

> Ashley compares the options to one another in terms of the profit that would be realized.
>
> Ashley compares the options to one another in terms of the cost of kitchen equipment.

Now the sentence completions read more smoothly.

The GMAT uses several different phrasings to refer generally to the entire set of options:

> . . . of each option
> . . . of the options being considered
> . . . of an option
> . . . of the various options
> . . . of the various options under consideration

The basic idea is that these phrases refer to each and every option.

Finally, (E)s are like chameleons. They can assume a phrasing that looks like any of the other categories:

> **120** — An (E) can assume a phrasing characteristic of any of the categories.

For example "Labor costs incurred in running a typical franchise restaurant" looks like either a (B) or a (C), but it appears nowhere in the passage. Though Ashley is concerned to keep her start-up costs to a minimum, she does not discuss ongoing costs so "labor costs" is an (E). Similarly, "Learning further theoretical business skills" sounds for all the world like an (A), but the passage states only that Ashley requires practical training and experience.

ATTACK STRATEGY FOR ANALYSIS OF SITUATIONS

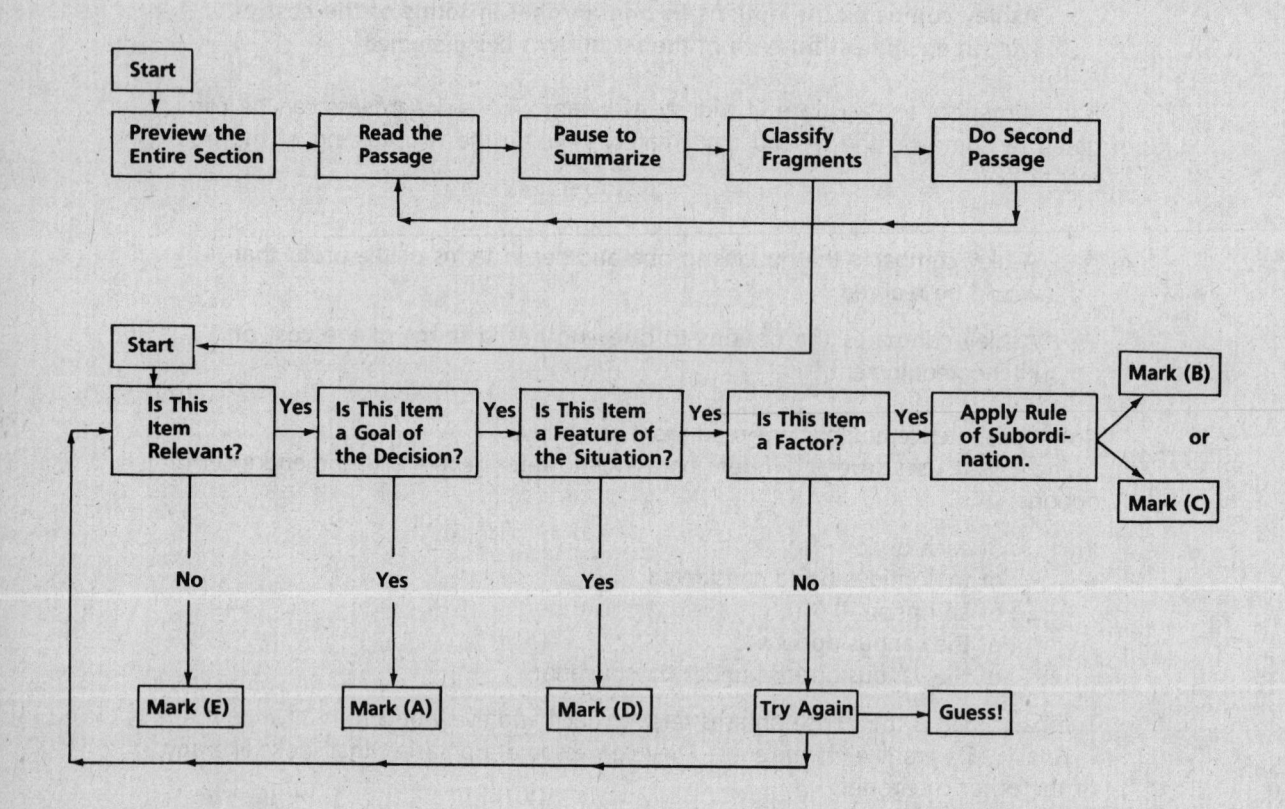

```
Start
  ↓
Preview the → Read the → Pause to → Classify → Do Second
Entire Section   Passage   Summarize   Fragments    Passage
```

```
Start
  ↓
Is This Item Relevant? —Yes→ Is This Item a Goal of the Decision? —Yes→ Is This Item a Feature of the Situation? —Yes→ Is This Item a Factor? —Yes→ Apply Rule of Subordination. → Mark (B) or Mark (C)
  ↓No                          ↓Yes                                      ↓Yes                                         ↓No
Mark (E)                     Mark (A)                                   Mark (D)                                     Try Again → Guess!
```

The standard GMAT analysis of situations section contains two decisional situations, each described in a passage of 900 to 1,100 words. Each passage is then followed by 17 or 18 fragments, so that there are 35 fragments in all in the entire section. The time limit to complete all work in the section is 30 minutes.

You begin your attack on the section with a preview:

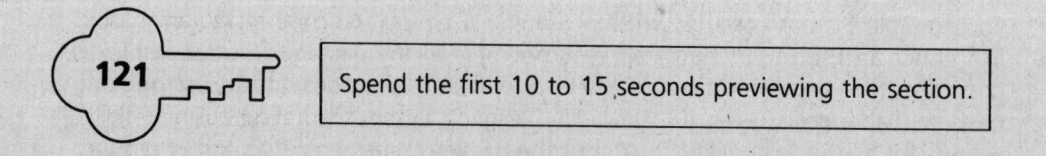

121 Spend the first 10 to 15 seconds previewing the section.

Turn quickly through the passages of the section to determine that you do, in fact,

Analysis of Situations / 117

have only two decisions to analyze and that they are approximately equal in length. We do not expect any variation in the format described; but the preview will alert you to any changes, so you can adjust your strategy accordingly. The passages are usually equal in length and difficulty, though the second one may be *slightly* more complicated than the first:

122 Plan to finish your work on the first passage in 13 to 14 minutes.

This will give you a small time reserve to be applied against the second passage should it turn out to be more difficult.

The GMAT has used the same set of directions for analysis of situations for years. It is 99.99 percent certain that these will not change, therefore:

123 Memorize the underlying meanings of the five categories.

You do not need to memorize the exact definitions, but you should know instinctively that a goal is an (A), a nonsubordinated factor is a (B), a subordinated factor is a (C), a structural feature is a (D), and anything else is an (E). In this way you will not waste time constantly consulting the directions.

The second step in the attack strategy is to read the passage. Since you plan to complete the first passage and fragments in 13 or 14 minutes, this means you must complete your reading of the passage proper in 5 or 6 minutes:

124 Finish your initial reading of the passage in 5 to 6 minutes.

This is not as difficult as it sounds. The typical passage is not more than 1,000 words long, and the average reading speed of a college graduate is well over 250 words per minute. Even assuming a slow rate (250 words per minute), the reading can be completed in only 4 minutes. There are several keys that will help you stay within this 5- to 6-minute time limit.

125 Do not be put off by the alien nature of the subject matter.

The subject matter of the decision is not likely to be familiar to you. Do not let this interfere with your reading. You do not need any technical information. Remember you are only interested in the logical structure of the passage, not in the specific technical content.

A corollary to this is:

> **126** Do not waste time trying to memorize details or unravel overly technical points.

You are allowed to go back to the passage while you are answering the questions in this section. It would be a waste of time and energy to memorize anything. Read for the overall picture.

We have previously noted some of the structural features of the typical passage. Now we will pinpoint those passing references in the form of keys:

> **127** Look for the point which marks the beginning of the discussion of the actual decision.

We pointed out that the first paragraph (or two) is likely to be introductory. This information is usually important only insofar as it provides you with the background you need to understand who the decision maker is and what events led up to the decisional situation. When you have reached that point, then begin to read for the logical structure of the decision:

> **128** Read for the logical structure of the decision; for example, structural features, goals, and factors. *Do not* try to read for (A)s, (D)s, (B)s, and (C)s.

Remember that there are many ways of phrasing the same fragment. Moreover, not every detail in the passage can be used in a list of only 17 or 18 fragments. It is not wise, therefore, to anticipate the wording of fragments that might appear. Rather, if you have understood the logic of the decision, you will be in a position to classify any fragment that appears no matter how it is worded.

After you have finished your reading, pause to summarize in your mind what you have read:

129 — Pause to answer for yourself: Who is the decision maker (are the decision makers)? What is the problem? What created the problem? What are the options? How does the decision maker (do the decision makers) compare one option to another?

This "reconstruction" step is important because the GMAT has different ways of developing passages. Some passages are written in the third person (ordinary narrative), others are written as the transcript of a group discussion with the various participants offering arguments for or against the options, still others are presented as documents (see the Ashley decision). No matter what the form of development may be, most GMAT passages contain a short paragraph (or a subpart of a paragraph) in which the decision maker summarizes some of the important points of the discussion:

130 — Look for a paragraph that summarizes the criteria by which the options are to be judged.

In the Ashley and the franchise restaurant decision, the third paragraph summarized the three criteria by which Ashley evaluated the desirability of the franchises, but such paragraphs can also appear toward the end of the passage. If there is such a paragraph in the passage, it will help you organize your analysis of the decision.

Having completed your logical summary of what you have read, you will proceed to answer fragments. Start with the first fragment in the list, and apply the next series of quesitons. First, ask whether the item is even relevant. If you have read carefully, you should be able to eliminate items that are just not relevant; and if an item is not relevant, there is no reason to worry about what it might have been; for example, a (B) or a (C), if it *had* been relevant.

If you decide the item is relevant, then you ask whether it is a goal, using the tests we have developed. If the item is a goal, answer (A); otherwise, ask the next question: is it a feature of the situation? Keeping in mind the three functions served by features of the situation and using the sentence completion test we have developed determine whether the item is a (D). If it is not, then ask whether the item is a factor. If you are sure it is a factor, then apply the rule of subordination to determine whether it is a (B) or a (C). If you are not sure whether it is a factor, then try again.

Of course, you cannot keep trying and trying. At some point you will have to make a guess and move on:

131 — In analysis of situations, *always* make a guess.

This advice is based on two premises. One, you will certainly be able to eliminate two or three of the choices, making a guess imperative. Two, you can make intelligent guesses based on the interplay of the fragments listed. In fact, you should be able to classify the following four fragments even though you know nothing about the situation on which they are based:

> Unsatisfactoriness of a system requiring overly extensive renovations
> Extent of renovations required under each of the proposed systems
> Relocation of stairwell required to implement a system of central dispersements
> A system that can be implemented without unnecessary renovation

The interplay of the fragments should suggest to you that one of the features of the structure of the decision is the necessity of avoiding extensive renovations. Thus the first fragment would be a (D). Further, this implies that finding a system that does not require extensive renovation is a goal, so the fourth fragment is an (A). Then, we know that the options will be compared in terms of the extent of renovation required, making the second fragment a (B), and the third a (C) as a part of it.

Occasionally, it will be difficult to distinguish whether a factor is intended to be a (B) or a (C). You may be able to use the interplay of fragments as an additional tool:

---

132 — When in doubt as to whether a fragment is a (B) or a (C), study the other fragments in the list.

If you find another fragment to which the one in question can be subordinated, then classify the doubtful fragment as (C); otherwise classify it as a (B) on the assumption that there is nothing to which it is subordinate. The rule is not foolproof, however, since there is no necessity for the GMAT to include in the list of fragments a (B) for all of the (C)s. Logically, of course, every (C) requires an overriding (B); but the question preparers may or may not elect to use the (B) in the list of fragments, although the (B) will virtually always appear if a (C) of that group appears. If this rule fails you, then:

---

133 — When in doubt as to whether a fragment is a (B) or a (C), answer (B) when the fragment refers to the entire set of options.

Again, this is not a first line of attack—only a rule for guessing.

Equipped with an understanding of how to analyze a decision backed up with these test-taking strategies, you should be able to enter an answer for every item in this section.

5.
READING COMPREHENSION

Reading comprehension tests reading comprehension, and with that vacuous statement you may think we have exhausted our supply of useful test-taking hints. Not so!

To be sure, reading skills develop over a long period; and, unlike the idea of a math or grammar review, the concept of a reading comprehension review seems silly. This chapter does not attempt such a review. Rather, this chapter is designed to help you adapt your already developed reading skills to the exam. It will help you learn to read for the test.

THE STRUCTURE OF A READING COMPREHENSION TEST

The first step in learning to read for the test is to become familiar with the structure of a reading comprehension exercise. On the Graduate Management Admission Test (GMAT), a reading comprehension exercise consists of a passage of approximately 550 words followed by seven to nine questions.

There are three features that characterize the passages: (1) topic, (2) format, and (3) density. First, the topics used on the exam range over many substantive areas, from literature to physics, from sociology to geology, from philosophy to biology. Consequently, though you may have some passing knowledge of the material discussed, the specific point made by the passage is not something you are likely to be familiar with:

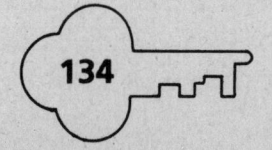

> **134** Do not expect to be familiar with the topic discussed in the passage.

121

The test writers go out of their way to find material that most students will not have seen before, for they want to avoid giving anyone an unfair advantage. Should you encounter material with which you are already familiar, consider that a bonus; but do not expect that you will. Reading comprehension is designed to test reading skills, not substantive knowledge.

Second, reading comprehension passages have the annoying feature that they begin seemingly in the middle of nowhere. Imagine starting to work on a passage that begins with the sentence:

> The basis of mutual understanding that, at the roots of the natural sciences is presupposed by participants in the processes of inquiry, is claimed by the cultural sciences as their authentic realm.

Your reaction is likely to be "What?" In fact, the passage in which this sentence appears treats a topic with which you probably do have some familiarity: to what extent are the behavioral sciences (e.g., sociology) like the hard sciences (e.g., physics). Although you may not remember any specifics about the debate, you probably read something about it in your introductory courses in college.

What makes this sentence, as an opening sentence, so jarring is that you lack a context. Think about the reading you are accustomed to doing. First, it is usually the case that it is something you have selected out of interest. You pick up a newspaper or a news magazine, and you read those articles that hold some intrinsic interest for you; for example, movie reviews but not sports. Second, the material has a context. For example, newspapers and news magazines use headlines. Before you begin to read, you know what the topic is. Our isolated sentence, above, would have been much less jarring had it been preceded by a headline:

Are Social Sciences Really Science?

Even this headline would be much less startling if you found it in what you knew to be an elementary sociology text. You might even have expected it. So our second point is this:

135 — Realize that you must begin reading without any point of reference.

Having no point of reference or context makes the task of reading much more difficult.

The third characteristic of the passages is density.

136 — Expect that the reading will be dry and often difficult.

These three features, choice of topic, method of presentation, and writing style, taken together, present another danger:

137 Do not let the reading comprehension passages intimidate you.

Having talked with thousands of test takers over the years, we have found that many students are simply intimidated by the passages. They know that they can read fairly well, but when they encounter a selection, the reading of which is made difficult by the features just described, they incorrectly attribute the cause of the difficulty to themselves, rather than to the structure of the exam. If you have ever taken this exam before, or some similar exam, and have had gnawing feelings of inadequacy ("These test people must be really smart to know all this stuff."), then you know about the intimidation. To combat the feeling of inadequacy, a feeling that can interfere with your performance in this section, just recall that the difficulty resides in the test, not you.

The second step in learning to read for the test is to become familiar with the types of questions used in reading comprehension. You may not be aware of the fact, but each question used in the reading comprehension test belongs to one of six types:

Main Idea Question

Each reading comprehension passage used on the exam is unified by some central theme, that is, the passage is written to make some main point. Main idea questions ask about this main point. They are often worded as follows:

Which of the following best describes the main point of the passage?
The primary purpose of the passage is to . . .
The author is primarily concerned with . . .
Which of the following titles best describes the content of the passage?

Supporting Idea Questions

These questions ask about details that are explicitly mentioned in the passage. A supporting idea is not the main idea, so this type differs from the first type of question just described. Additionally, the ideas used by the author to support the main point are explicitly mentioned by the author. So supporting idea questions differ from the next category, implied idea questions. Supporting idea questions are often worded as follows:

According to the passage. . . .
The author mentions. . . .
Which of the following questions does the author answer in the passage?

Implied Idea Questions

These are to be distinguished from supporting idea questions in that they are not explicitly stated in the passage but are strongly implied in the passage. Often, an author will make a point by suggestion rather than by explicit statement. These questions ask about such meaning. Be assured, however, that the inferences needed to answer such questions are not long chains of reasoning. Instead, you will be asked to go only one step beyond the literal meaning of the passage. For example, if the passage explicitly makes a statement of the form "A phenomenon X is always followed by phenomenon Y," you might be asked to infer what has happened if Y did not occur. If Y did not occur, we can infer that X did not occur. Implied idea questions are often worded as follows:

>It can be inferred from the passage that . . .
>It can be inferred that which of the following . . .
>The author implies that . . .
>The author uses the phrase ". . ." to mean . . .

Logical Structure Questions

As we have noted, the passage constitutes a unified whole, that is, a central thesis supported logically by explicit points. Logical structure questions ask about the way the passage is put together. A logical structure question might ask about the overall logical development of the passage. In that case, it would resemble a main idea question, but its emphasis would be the form of the passage rather than the content. This type of logical structure question is often phrased as follows:

>The development of the passage is primarily . . .
>The author develops the passage primarily by . . .

Other logical structure questions are concerned with the role played by supporting ideas. These questions resemble supporting idea questions, but their emphasis is not so much *what* the author explicitly said as *why* the author said it. Such questions are often phrased as follows:

>The author cites ". . ." primarily in order to. . . .
>The author mentions ". . ." in order to. . . .

Further Application Questions

These questions ask that you abstract from the specific content and apply the author's ideas to a new situation. The further application question may be the most difficult of the six types, because it asks that you go beyond what is explicitly mentioned and even beyond what is strongly implied. Further application questions present situations different from those mentioned in the text. These questions are often phrased as follows:

> With which of the following conclusions would the author be most likely to agree?
>
> With which of the following statements would the author be *least* likely to agree?
>
> Which of the following statements, if true, would most weaken the conclusion that . . . ?
>
> Which of the following would be a logically appropriate topic for the author to take up in the next paragraph to continue the passage?

Attitude Questions

These questions ask that you draw some conclusion about the author's attitude toward a subject or about the author's style. You will use clues in the passage, such as adjectives used by the author, to determine whether the author is supportive, critical, disinterested, etc. These questions are often phrased as follows:

> The tone of the author's closing remarks can best be described as . . .
> The tone of the passage can best be described as . . .
> The author's attitude toward . . . can best be described as . . .

These, then, are the six types of questions used in the reading comprehension part of the test. There is one final point to be made about the structure of this question type: the answer choices. As test takers, we are usually preoccupied with the correct choice. For the test writers, the wrong answers are very important, for the wrong answers must be wrong, yet they must also appear to be at least plausible. In fact, in test writers' parlance, the wrong choices are often referred to as "distractors." This does not mean they are included as tricks, but it does mean that the wrong answers must not be so obviously wrong as to make the right choice stand out like a neon sign.

This feature of the test introduces yet another difficulty that you must learn to cope with. The answer choices are often very similar, and you must read them very carefully. The exam differs from nonmultiple-choice exams in this respect. Recall the tests given in freshman survey courses. They usually contain questions such as: "What was the date of the first Council of Nicea?" You are to supply the answer, and the answer will be very short.

If you look at a typical reading comprehension exercise, you will see that there are nearly as many words in the answer choices as there are in the passage itself. This should give you some idea of the importance of attending carefully to the answer choices as well as the passage and the question stems.

READING THE PASSAGE

We have indicated some of the difficulties you are likely to encounter in reading a passage. Now we will discuss some techniques for overcoming those difficulties.

In general, we may say that reading comprehension requires that you *understand* and *evaluate* the passage, but there are levels of understanding and evaluation. Obviously, there are times when you need only a general understanding of what you are reading, and other times when you need a more precise understanding. Sometimes you are required to be very critical of written material; on other occasions it is sufficient that you understand it. Taking our clue from the structure of a reading comprehension exercise, we ask: what do you need to learn from the passage?

We identify four levels of understanding and evaluation. (1) You must have an understanding of the overall idea or main point of the passage. Not only will you need this information to answer any main idea question, you cannot hope to make sense of the material unless you understand the overall development. (2) You must have a general understanding of the content and substructure of the passage; that is, you must read and comprehend the specific ideas and appreciate the role they play in the overall development. (3) It may be necessary to subject some of the specific ideas to closer scrutiny, to ask, for example, exactly what does the author mean or what precise role does this piece of information play. (4) There is a level of understanding and evaluation that moves beyond the explicit. At this level you are asking, for example, what further conclusions might be drawn from this information.

These four levels are not completely independent of one another, and a good reader is likely to work on all four levels simultaneously. Still, there is a certain priority to the levels. You need the overall understanding of the first level to make sense of the general understanding of the second level. You need the general understanding of the second level for the very precise understanding of the third level. You need the full understanding of the overall structure, general ideas, and specific details to reach conclusions on the fourth level.

Further, as a matter of answering questions, the first and second levels are absolutely critical. The third and fourth levels become important only insofar as the test presents questions that require such a deep understanding. By this we mean that without the first two levels, comprehension never gets off the ground, but the third and fourth levels are called into play by specific test questions.

These observations will help you organize your reading. Your reading of the passage should aim at the overall and general understanding of ideas. Then, the specific questions will guide you in determining what ideas need further study. After all, you could not hope to list all of the additional inferences that might be drawn or further applications that could be made. But you do not have to. You are responsible only for those that appear as questions.

The first step in reading is to grasp the overall idea of the passage. Remember that the passage will seem to start in the middle of nowhere. We suggest:

138 — Begin your reading by previewing the first sentence of each paragraph.

The first sentence of a paragraph is often the topic sentence, and reading the topic sentences of the three or four paragraphs in the passage will give you some idea of the general subject matter of the passage. Then, as you read,

> **139** Consciously ask yourself "What is the point the author is ultimately trying to make?"

This will serve as the principle of organization. It will allow you to make sense of the subordinate ideas in the passage.

For the subordinate ideas, as you read through the passage, you should

> **140** Consciously ask why the author has introduced each major idea.

That is, you ask what relationship does it have to the main thesis. Notice that this is the level of general understanding. Do not try to go so far as to evaluate, that is, attack or defend, the argument. That level can wait for later.

If you come across material that seems difficult to understand, do not belabor it. Once you understand the logical function it serves in the overall development, move on:

> **141** Bracket, mentally or in writing, material that is very technical or difficult to understand.

If some question depends on your understanding the technical information, you can go back and decipher it.

Finally, when you reach the end of your reading, pause to summarize the main points in your mind:

> **142** Before attempting to answer the questions, quickly review the structure of the passage.

Let us apply this to a passage:

Desertification in the arid United States is flagrant. Groundwater supplies beneath vast stretches of land are dropping precipitously. Whole river systems have dried up; others are choked with sediment washed from denuded land. Hundreds of thousands of acres of previously irrigated cropland have been abandoned to wind or weeds. Several million acres of natural grassland are eroding at unnaturally high rates as a result of cultivation or overgrazing. All told about 225 million acres of land are undergoing severe desertification.

Federal subsidies encourage the exploitation of arid land resources. Low-interest loans for irrigation and other water delivery systems encourage farmers, industry, and municipalities to mine groundwater. Federal disaster relief and commodity programs encourage arid land farmers to plow up natural grassland to plant crops such as wheat, and especially, cotton. Federal grazing fees that are well below the free market price encourage overgrazing of the commons. The market also provides powerful incentives to exploit arid land resources beyond their carrying capacity. When commodity prices are high relative to the farmer's or rancher's operating costs, the return on a production-enhancing investment is invariably greater than the return on a conservation investment. And when commodity prices are relatively low, arid land ranchers and farmers often have to use all their available financial resources to stay solvent.

The incentives to exploit arid land resources are greater today than ever. The government is now offering huge new subsidies to produce synfuel from coal or oil shale as well as alcohol fuel from crops. Moreover, commodity prices are on the rise; and they will provide farmers and agribusiness with powerful incentives to overexploit arid land resources. The existing federal government cost-share programs designed to help finance the conservation of soil, water, and vegetation pale in comparison to such incentives.

In the final analysis, when viewed in the national perspective, the effects on agriculture are the most troublesome aspect of desertification in the United States. For it comes at a time when we are losing over a million acres of rain-watered crop and pasture land per year to "higher uses"—shopping centers, industrial parks, housing developments, and waste dumps—heedless of the economic need of the United States to export agricultural products or of the world's need for U.S. food and fiber. Today the arid West accounts for 20 percent of the nation's total agricultural output. If the United States is, as it appears, well on its way toward overdrawing the arid land resources, then the policy choice is simply to pay now for the appropriate remedies or pay far more later, when productive benefits from arid land resources have been both realized and largely terminated.

The first sentences of each of the four paragraphs should give you a good idea of what the author is discussing: desertification. And it appears from these sentences that desertification has to do with farming dry lands. We also learn that the author is discussing some of the dangers of desertification and government policies that affect desertification.

Now you return to the first paragraph. The remainder of paragraph 1 amplifies the idea of the opening sentence. It explains further the process of desertification and highlights the extent of the problem. That is all you need to learn from the first paragraph.

The second paragraph begins by noting that federal subsidies encourage exploitation of arid land. Then, it goes on to describe federal policies that encourage desertification: low-interest loans for irrigation, disaster relief, commodities programs, and grazing fees. The author also notes that market forces contribute to the problem. In your first reading, you might or might not study the idea of market forces in greater detail. For most people the discussion of the relationship between market prices and agricultural investment would require the third level of understanding. If this is true for you, the better policy would be to place that materially in mental (or even written) brackets. You would say to yourself, "Market incentives also contribute . . . I will come back and study the last half of paragraph 2 in greater detail if I need to in order to answer a question on this part of the passage."

The third paragraph begins by stating that incentives to exploit arid land are greater than ever before. The second sentence points out that there are additional government incentives to do so. The third sentences refers, once again, to the market forces. Again, it may be necessary to bracket this idea.

The fourth paragraph begins with a statement that the desertification poses a serious threat to agriculture. What is the nature of that threat? According to the second sentence, we are already losing crop and pasture land to other uses. What will be the consequence of this loss? Inability to produce agricultural products. What can be done? According to the author, we must pay for the appropriate remedies.

At this juncture, you would want to stop and do a mental summary. On paper this summary would look like this:

Overall Idea: Desertification Is a Serious Problem That Must Be Faced.

I. Desertification is flagrant (with examples).
II. Economic forces encourage desertification.
   A. Federal subsidies (with examples).
   B. Market forces (explanation bracketed).
III. Forces push toward desertification more strongly.
   A. Federal programs (with examples).
   B. Market forces (explanation bracketed).
IV. Desertification has bad effects.
   A. We are losing land in other ways.
   B. Desertification will inhibit agricultural production.

Now, we have the framework we need to understand the questions. If we need to return to the passage for clarification or further information, we are at liberty to do so. Consider some possible questions:

The author is primarily concerned with

(A) discussing a solution
(B) describing a problem
(C) replying to a detractor
(D) finding a contradiction
(E) defining a term

The correct answer is (B). (C) and (D) can be eliminated because the author never refers to a detractor or a contradiction. (E) is incorrect since whatever definition of desertification is offered implicitly in the passage is incidental to the larger discussion of its causes and effects. (A) is the second best answer. There is some hint as to what the author would recommend as a solution in the final paragraph, but outlining a solution is not the overall thesis of the passage. (B) nicely describes the overall point of the passage, which is to discuss a problem.

The author's attitude toward desertification can best be described as one of

(A) alarm

(B) optimism
(C) understanding
(D) conciliation
(E) concern

The correct answer is (E). (B) can be eliminated since our reading of the passage shows that the author is opposed to desertification. (C) can be eliminated since the author's treatment presupposes that he understands the process of desertificaiton, but the treatment goes beyond mere understanding. (D) can be eliminated for the same reason as (B). Finally, our choice is between (A) and (E). Both have merit in that they capture the negative aspect of the author's attitude, but (A) overstates the case. While the author's treatment is one of concern, it does not reach the level of alarm.

The passage mentions all of the following as effects of desertification except:

(A) increased sediments in rivers
(B) erosion of land
(C) overcultivation of arid land
(D) decreasing groundwater supplies
(E) loss of land to wind or weeds

This is an explicit idea question. You need only return to the passage to check which of the choices were mentioned as effects of desertification. (A), (B), (D), and (E) were all mentioned as *effects*, but (C) was mentioned not as an effect but as a *cause* of desertification.

According to the passage, the first serious effect of desertification would be the reduced ability of

(A) the United States to continue to export agricultural products
(B) municipalities to supply water to meet the needs of residents
(C) farmers to cover the cost of producing crops
(D) the United States to meet the food needs of its own people
(E) the United States to produce sufficient fuel for energy

The answer to this explicit idea question is found in the fourth paragraph. Based on our first reading, we should be able to eliminate (B), (C), and (E); but (A) and (D) seem relatively close. At this juncture, we must descend to that third level of reading. From our first reading we learned that desertification will interfere with agricultural productivity in some way, but that general understanding is not sufficient to answer this question. Now we need a more precise understanding of the specific detail. Consulting the fourth paragraph, we find the information we need: the first serious effect is likely to be reduced ability to export.

It can be inferred from the passage that farmers invest in production enhancing equipment when

(A) the government subsidizes the purchase
(B) demand for commodities is slack
(C) profits on commodities are high
(D) farmers are close to insolvency
(E) lands are purchased for nonagricultural uses

The correct answer to this implied idea question is (C), and to answer it, we must return to the material we bracketed in paragraph 2. There the author notes that when commodities prices are high relative to production costs, the farmers invest in equipment to expand production. We infer, therefore, that farmers are attracted by the prospect of high profits.

The passage leads most logically to a discussion of a proposal for

(A) reduced agricultural output in the United States
(B) direct government aid to farmers affected by desertification
(C) curtailing the conversion of land to shopping centers and housing
(D) government assistance to develop farming methods to increase exploitation of arid land
(E) increased government assistance to finance the conservation of arid land

The correct answer to this question is (E), and to answer it we must descend to the deepest level of reading. The author indicates that government programs which encourage exploitation of arid land are in large part responsible for the rapid rate of desertification. A natural extension of the discussion would be a proposal for government spending to conserve arid lands, and this receives specific support in the third paragraph where the author states that government conservation incentives are inadequate. With regard to (A), the author must believe it is necessary for the United States to continue to export agricultural products for he favors conserving arid land while meeting this demand. (B) is surely incorrect for the author argues that aid to farmers is one cause of rapid desertification. (D) is incorrect for the same reason. As for (C), the conversion of land to so-called higher uses is mentioned as a factor complicating the ill-effects of desertification—not a cause of desertification itself. Keeping all of this in mind, it would seem that the most natural extension of the passage would be a proposal for combating desertification.

ANSWERING THE QUESTIONS

Now we will take a closer look at the pattern to the incorrect choices for each of the six question types. The following passage will be the basis for the questions:

At the present time, 98 percent of the world energy consumption comes from stored sources, such as fossil fuels or nuclear fuel. Only hydroelectric and wood energy represent completely renewable sources on ordinary time scales. Discovery of large additional fossil fuel reserves, solution of the nuclear safety and waste disposal problems, or the development of controlled thermonuclear fusion will provide only a short-term solution to the world's energy crisis. Within about 100 years, the thermal pollution resulting from our increased energy consumption will make solar energy a necessity at any cost.

Man's energy consumption is currently about 1 part in 10,000 that of the energy we receive from the sun. However, it is growing at a 5 percent rate, of which about 2 percent represents a population growth and 3 percent a per capita energy increase. If this growth continues, within 100 years our energy consumption will be about 1 percent of the absorbed solar energy, enough to increase the average temperature of the earth by about 1° Centigrade if stored energy continues to be our predominant source. This will be the point at which there will be significant effects on our climate, including the melting of the polar ice caps, a phenomenon which will raise the level of the oceans and flood parts of our major cities. There is positive feedback associated with this process, since the polar ice cap contributes to the partial reflectivity of the energy arriving from the sun: as the ice caps begin to melt, the reflectivity will decrease, thus heating the earth still further.

It is often stated that the growth rate will decline or that energy conservation measures will preclude any long-range problem. Instead, this only postpones the problem by a few years. Conservation by a factor of two together with a maintenance of the 5 percent growth rate delays the problem by only 14 years. Reduction of the growth rate to 4 percent postpones the problem by only 25 years; in addition the inequities in standards of living throughout the world will provide pressure toward an increase in growth rate particularly if cheap energy is available. The problem of changing climate will not be evident until perhaps 10 years before it becomes critical due to the nature of an exponential growth rate together with the normal annual weather variations. This may be too short a period to circumvent the problem by converting to other energy sources, so advance planning is a necessity.

The only practical means of avoiding the problem of thermal pollution appears to be the use of solar energy. (Schemes to "air condition" the earth do not appear to be feasible before the 22nd century.) Using solar energy before it is dissipated to heat does not increase the earth's energy balance. The cost of solar energy is extremely favorable now, particularly when compared to the cost of relocating many of our major cities.

Main Idea Questions

There are three main forms for main idea questions:

Which of the following best describes the main point of the passage?
The author is primarily concerned to . . .
Which of the following titles best describes the content of the passage?

Despite the variation, the key to a main idea question is this:

143 For a main idea question, select an answer choice which refers to all of the important aspects in the passage without going beyond the scope of the passage.

Consider an example of the first sort:

> Which of the following best describes the main point of the passage?
>
> (A) The problem of thermal pollution cannot be solved by energy conservation measures.
> (B) Thermal pollution will continue to increase dangerously unless new energy sources are found.
> (C) Solar energy is the only practical way to avoid a catastrophe caused by thermal pollution.
> (D) Thermal pollution is the result of releasing more stored energy than is dissipated into space.
> (E) Man's careless use of the environment now poses a serious threat to the balance of nature.

The correct answer is (C). There are two aspects to the main point of this passage: (1) the danger posed by thermal pollution and (2) solar energy as the only solution to the problem. (A), (B), and (D) are not correct answers to this main idea because they are too limited. They refer to parts of the passage or aspects of the argument; but a part or an aspect is not the central thesis. On the other side, (E) is incorrect because its description goes beyond the scope of the passage. The author is specifically concerned with thermal pollution and its effects—not with pollution and the balance of nature generally. (C), however, neatly describes both aspects of the central thesis.

> The author is primarily concerned to
>
> (A) criticize people who oppose conversion to solar energy
> (B) argue for increased use of solar energy
> (C) refute arguments against the practicality of solar energy
> (D) expose the fallacy behind arguments for conservation
> (E) discuss the dangers of thermal pollution

The correct answer to this main idea question is (B). (E) can be eliminated since it refers to only half of the main thesis, as discussed above. (A) can be eliminated since the author does not criticize people. Rather, he offers arguments for solar energy. (C) is incorrect because the author does not cite any such arguments for refutation. (D) is incorrect, for to the extent that the author does argue that conservation by itself will not solve thermal pollution, this is only one aspect of the passage.

There is a further point to be made about a question of this form:

> **144** With a main idea question of sentence completion format, be sure to test the suitability of the first word of each choice.

In this case, the first words of (A), (C), and (D) just do not do justice to the passage. The author is not concerned to criticize, to refute, or to expose.

> Which of the following titles best describes the content of the passage?

(A) Thermal Pollution and the Need for Solar Energy
(B) The Inadequacy of Conservation as a Solution to Thermal Pollution
(C) Pollution and the Danger of Man's Environment
(D) Government Policies that Encourage Thermal Pollution
(E) Impracticality of Air Conditioning the Earth

(B) and (E) are inadequate as titles because they refer only to parts of the passage. (C) and (D) can be eliminated because they go beyond the discussion of solar energy as the solution to thermal pollution. (A), however, does the job by referring to the two aspects of the passage mentioned above: thermal pollution and the need for solar energy.

Supporting Idea Questions

Remember that supporting idea questions are questions about ideas explicitly mentioned in the passage. Often answers to supporting idea questions are wrong because they are not explicitly mentioned in the text:

145 — For a supporting idea question, exclude answer choices that are not mentioned in the passage or go beyond the scope of the passage.

According to the passage, thermal pollution is caused by

(A) increased use of automobiles by affluent nations
(B) releasing more stored solar energy than is dissipated
(C) industries which pursue profits without concern for the environment
(D) opposition to conversion to new energy sources such as solar energy
(E) inaccuracies in scientific measurement of levels of dangerous emissions

The correct answer to this question is (B), and the remaining choices can be eliminated because they simply are not mentioned in the passage. The answer to a supporting idea question is always somewhere in the text.

Although the correct answer to a supporting idea question will be found in the text, many other ideas are also found in the text:

146 — For a supporting idea question, make sure you find the part of the passage that has the information for that question.

Often, the wrong answer to a supporting idea question is something actually mentioned in the text, but at a point that is not relevant to the question being answered:

> The positive feedback mentioned in the second paragraph means that the melting of the polar ice caps will
>
> (A) reduce per capita energy consumption
> (B) accelerate the transition to solar energy
> (C) intensify the effects of thermal pollution
> (D) necessitate a shift to alternative energy sources
> (E) result in the innundation of major cities

The correct answer to the question can be found by locating the discussion of polar ice caps. At the end of the second paragraph, the author notes that there is a positive feedback associated with the melting of the polar ice caps: as the ice caps melt, the less solar energy they reflect, the higher the temperature, and so the more the ice caps melt. This is correctly described by choice (C). Answer (E) is mentioned only in the fourth paragraph as the general effect of thermal pollution, so it is not going to be the correct idea for a supporting idea question aimed at the second paragraph. Answer (D) describes the main point of the passage, but the main point of the passage will not be the correct answer to a supporting idea question. (A) and (B) use language that appears in the passage, but (A) and (B) do not answer the question asked.

Some supporting idea questions use thought reversers, such as not, but, or except:

> **147** If a supporting idea question contains a thought reverser, the correct answer will either not be mentioned in the passage or, if mentioned, will not be responsive.

> According to the passage, all of the following are factors which will tend to increase thermal pollution *except*
>
> (A) the earth's increasing population
> (B) melting of the polar ice caps
> (C) increase in per capita energy consumption
> (D) pressure to redress standard of living inequities by increasing energy consumption
> (E) expected anomalies in weather patterns

(A), (B), and (C) are mentioned in the second paragraph as contributing to thermal pollution. (D) is mentioned in the third paragraph as a pressure increasing thermal polution. (E) is mentioned in the third paragraph—but not as a factor contributing to thermal pollution. Unpredictable weather patterns make it difficult to predict when thermal pollution will reach the critical level, but the weather patterns are not said to contribute to thermal pollution.

Implied Idea Questions

These ask that you draw an inference based on information provided in the passage, but remember

> **148** The correct answer to an implied idea question will be only one step removed from what is explicitly stated in the text.

It can be inferred that air conditioning the earth refers to proposals to

(A) distribute frigid air from the polar ice caps to coastal cities
(B) dissipate stored solar energy released through energy consumption into space
(C) conserve completely renewable resources by requiring that they be replaced as quickly as they are consumed
(D) avoid further thermal pollution by converting to solar energy
(E) utilize hydroelectric and wood energy to replace nonconventional energy sources such as nuclear energy

In the final paragraph, the author refers to the possibility of air conditioning the earth, a phrase placed in quotation marks, which indicates that the use is nonstandard. Ordinarily, we use air conditioning to refer to the process of cooling a room or a building. Obviously, the author is not referring to some gigantic air-conditioning unit mounted on the top of the earth. But the general idea of removing heat seems to be what the term means in this context. Thermal pollution is the buildup of energy, and we are showing a positive buildup because fossil fuel and other sources of energy release energy which was previously stored. So this, coupled with the sun's energy, gives us a positive (though not desirable) balance of energy retention over loss. The idea of air conditioning the earth, though not feasible according to the passage, must refer to schemes to get rid of this energy, say into outer space. This is the idea presented in (B), and you will notice that it is only one step removed from the text. As for (A), redistribution of thermal energy within the earth's energy system will not solve the problem of accumulated energy, so that cannot be what proponents of air conditioning have in mind. So (E) must be incorrect too, for burning more fuel will not cool the earth.

(C) and (D) are wrong for similar reasons:

> **149** For implied idea questions, eliminate any answer choice that makes a reasonable statement that is not responsive to the question.

Whereas (A) and (E) make unreasonable statements, both (C) and (D) are at least consistent with the spirit of the passage. (C) and (D), however reasonable they may be, do not constitute responses to the question. (C) is a good definition of conservation, but not air conditioning. (D) is the recommendation given by the author, but it is not a response to this question.

Logical Structure Questions

We mentioned that logical structure questions may focus either upon the overall logical structure of the passage or on the role played by some detail. If the question is about the overall logical structure of the passage, treat the question as you would a main idea question:

> **150** The correct answer to a question that asks about the overall development of a passage will correctly describe in general terms the most important aspects of the development without referring to extraneous material.

The author is primarily concerned with

(A) describing a phenomenon and explaining its causes
(B) outlining a position and supporting it with statistics
(C) isolating an ambiguity and clarifying it by definition
(D) presenting a problem and advocating a solution for it
(E) citing a counterargument and refuting it

The correct answer is (D). The author does two things in the passage: He *describes* the problem of thermal pollution and he *advocates* solar energy as a solution. (A) is incorrect for though the author does describe the phenomenon of thermal pollution and its causes, he also proposes a solution. (B) is incorrect since it fails to make reference to the fact that an important part of the passage is the description of a problem. (C) is partially correct. The author has a position, but (D) better describes the twofold nature of that position. It refers more precisely to the fact that the author's position includes presenting a problem and advocating a solution.

Other logical structure questions ask about the logical role played by a supporting detail. This type of logical structure question is similar to the supporting detail question, but here the question is not whether the author mentioned something—that is taken for granted. The question starts from the assumption that the idea was mentioned by the author and proceeds to ask why it was mentioned.

> **151** With a question that asks about the logical function of a detail, locate the appropriate reference and analyze *why* the author introduced the point at just that juncture.

The author mentions the possibility of energy conservation in paragraph 3 in order to

(A) preempt and refute a possible objection to his position
(B) support directly the central thesis of the passage
(C) minimize the significance of a contradiction in the passage
(D) prove that such measures are ineffective and counterproductive
(E) supply the reader with additional background information

The correct answer to the question is (A). This question differs from a supporting idea question in that it acknowledges that the idea is explicitly mentioned in the third paragraph. We go, then, to the third paragraph and locate the needed material. Why does the author discuss energy conservation at this particular point? Because conservation may seem to some readers to be an alternative to solar energy. The author argues against this idea. He says that a closer examination shows that conservation cannot avert but only postpone the crisis. In terms of forensic tactics, the author's move is to raise a possible objection and give an answer to it. (B) is incorrect, because the refutation of a possible objection does not support the central thesis *directly*, only *indirectly* by eliminating a possible counterargument. (C) is incorrect since the author never acknowledges he has fallen into any contradiction. (D) is incorrect since it overstates the case. The author admits that conservation has beneficial effects, but he denies that conservation obviates the need for solar energy. Finally, (E) is incorrect since the point is argumentative and not merely informational.

Further Application Questions

These are probably the most difficult questions in reading comprehension because they take you the farthest beyond the explicit text. As such, the correct choice is only tenuously related to the passage:

152 For a further application question, find the answer choice that has the most connection with the text.

Which of the following would be the most logical topic for the author to address in a succeeding paragraph?

(A) The problems of nuclear safety and waste disposal
(B) A history of the development of solar energy
(C) The availability and cost of solar energy technology
(D) The practical effects of flooding of coastal cities
(E) The feasibility of geothermic energy

Notice that the question asks "which of the *following* would be the *most logical* topic . . . ?" There is no reason the author could not proceed to discuss any topic at all—including his childhood, the Yankees' chances to win the pennant, or how to cook in a wok. But we are given only five choices, so we are in essence asked, which of the five choices has the closest connection to the text.

The correct answer is (C). Since the author has urged us to adopt solar energy, an appropriate continuation would be a discussion of how to implement solar energy. And (C) would be part of this discussion. (B) can be eliminated since the proposal depends upon the cost and feasibility of solar energy, not on the history of solar energy. (A) and (E) can be eliminated since the author has explicitly asserted that *only* solar energy will solve the problem of thermal pollution. Finally, (D) is incorrect since the author need not regale us with the gory details of this situation. He has already made the point. As readers, we will want to see the practical details of his plan to avoid the disaster.

Attitude Questions

In contrast to further application questions, these tend to be fairly easy:

153 — For an attitude question, arrange the answer choices as a continuum and pinpoint the author's attitude.

The tone of the passage is best described as one of

(A) unmitigated outrage
(B) cautious optimism
(C) reckless abandon
(D) smug self-assurance
(E) unqualified alarm

The correct answer is (B). The author describes a very dangerous situation. Reactions to a dangerous situation might run from strong, such as panic, through weak, such as indifference, to strong on the other side, such as confidence:

Panic ⟶ Worry ⟶ Indifference ⟶ Confidence

In this case, the author recognizes the problem, but he is hopeful or optimistic that solar energy will solve the problem. (A) is incorrect since the tone is not one of outrage. Though the author may be distressed at what he perceives to be the short-sightedness of policymakers, this distress does not color his writing. (C) is totally inappropriate since the author is analytical. (D) is inconsistent with the element of concern. Finally, (E) overstates the case. The author is not in a state of panic.

READING COMPREHENSION ATTACK STRATEGY

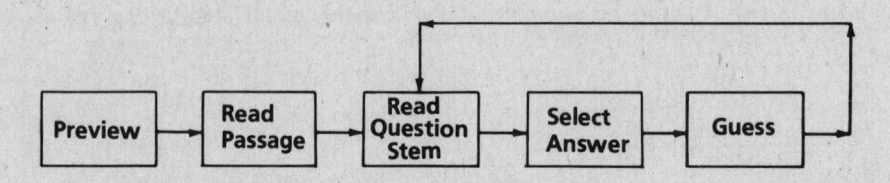

```
Preview → Read Passage → Read Question Stem → Select Answer → Guess
                              ↑_____|
```

This flow-chart outlines the steps you will take in attacking the reading comprehension section. The idea behind the method is obvious, but we want to make a comment or two about each step.

First, as we have already mentioned, you should preview the reading selection. Then we suggest:

154 You may find it useful to read the question stems before reading the passage.

Note that we have said this "may" be useful. Many people find that reading the question stems in advance performs a function similar to that served by the preview of the topic sentences. Others find this counterproductive. If you do decide to include question stems in your preview, do not include the answer choices. The answer choices would not be likely to add anything to the preview, and it would be time consuming to include them. Moreover, not every question stem will provide useful information. A question stem such as "All of the following factors will tend to increase thermal pollution *except*" tells you that the author will discuss thermal pollution and that thermal pollution is likely to increase. But a question stem such as "The main purpose of the passage is to" is purely formal and contains no useful information.

The next step is to read the passage using the techniques outlined in this chapter:

155 Reading comprehension is not an exercise in speed reading.

In fact, even reading at a fairly slow rate, say 250 words per minute, you will finish a 550-word passage in just over 2 minutes. Still, you cannot afford to get bogged down in the reading. The reading keys we have presented, particularly the key on bracketing, will help you move quickly through the passage:

156 — Finish reading the 550-word passage in 2 to 3 minutes.

This is necessary to leave time to answer the questions.

The third step is to read the first question stem. With regard to the question stem, there are two points to keep in mind. First:

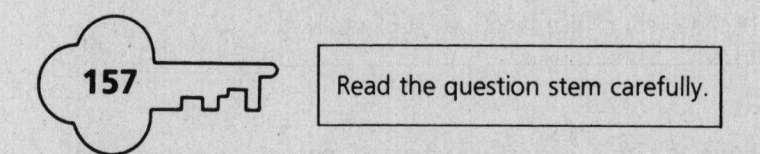

157 — Read the question stem carefully.

This is the reading comprehension part of the test, and understanding precisely what is asked for in a question is part of comprehension.

158 — Circle any thought reverser in the question stem.

A thought reverser is a word such as "not," "but," or "except" that transforms the question. Instead of looking for the ordinary answer, you will be looking for the exception—the answer that, under ordinary circumstances, would be incorrect. Because of time pressure, you may forget that there is a thought reverser in the stem. If you circle it, the mark will call itself to your attention.

As you read the question stem, you should also be making a note of any information included in the question that could help you in interpreting the meaning of the passage or that could help you in answering another question:

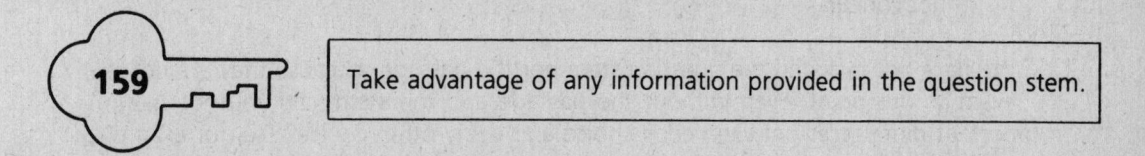

159 — Take advantage of any information provided in the question stem.

For example, consider this question stem:

> It can be inferred from the passage that the most important reason a general index of welfare cannot be designed . . .

This tells you that the author of the passage believes that a general index of welfare is not feasible. That could help you answer a later question:

142 / *101 Tips for Scoring High on the GMAT*

The author regards the idea of a general index of welfare as

(A) an unrealistic dream
(B) a scientific reality
(C) an important contribution
(D) a future necessity
(E) a desirable change

Since the first question stem states that the author regards the idea of a general index of welfare as unfeasible, we have the answer to the second question, choice (A).

The fourth step is to select an answer to the question:

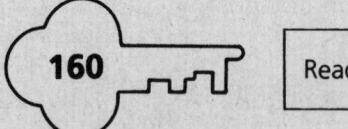

160 — Read every choice, and read it carefully.

To determine which answer choice is correct you may be required to read on the deepest levels mentioned above. A technique that will help you achieve the depth of comprehension required is to:

161 — Consciously contrast answer choices and study the differences among them.

As we have remarked elsewhere, one feature of the multiple-choice format is that the correct answer is included in the test booklet. Your task is to find it. You might, for example, have an array of answer choices such as these:

(A) A director and an actor agree on the interpretation of the character.
(B) Two directors cannot agree on an interpretation of the character.
(C) Each actor offers a different interpretation of the character.
(D) Two actors agree on an interpretation of the character.
(E) Two actors agree on an interpretation of the character, but the director does not concur.

We have not included the question stem nor the passage, because they are not relevant to our point. Even without the passage and the stem, can you not see important differences between each choice and every other choice? (A), for example, says that the answer to the question lies in the agreement between a director and an actor. (B) states that the answer is the disagreement of two directors—and so on. One such difference will be the important difference.

There is a final note regarding the answer choices:

162 — The best answer may not be the perfect answer.

Remember that the correct answer is judged only in the context of four other choices. The correct answer will be the best of the five, not necessarily the one you would have written. If you find yourself clearly favoring a choice but balking at finally selecting it because, you think, "It is not exactly right," remember that it does not have to be *exactly* right, it only has to be the *best* available.

The final step is guessing. You will surely be able to eliminate some answer choices as definitely incorrect. When you have done so but do not see the possibility of any further progress, make your guess, leave the question, and move to the next question. Repeat the process by reading the question stem, etc. When you have finished the exercise, go on to the next set of questions. Or if you have finished all of the questions in the section, go back and check your work.

6. SENTENCE CORRECTION

ANATOMY OF A SENTENCE CORRECTION ITEM

Sentence correction items require that you correct errors in a written sentence. The question stem will be a sentence all or part of which has been underlined. The answer choices represent alternative ways of rendering the underlined part:

Question 6-1

It should be emphasized that, contrary to common opinion, undercapitalization, not management errors, *are the most important cause* of failure of small businesses.

(A) are the most important cause
(B) are the more important cause
(C) is the most important cause
(D) is the most important causes
(E) is the more important cause

Answer choice (A) always reiterates the original sentence, and each of the remaining choices represents an alternative way of rendering the sentence.

The correct answer is to be determined by the following criterion:

> **163** If the underlined part of the sentence contains an error, the correct answer choice is the one that corrects the error without introducing a new error or changing the meaning of the sentence. If the original sentence is correct, (A) is the correct choice.

The correct answer to *Question 6-1* is (C). The sentence as originally presented does contain an error. The subject of the sentence is "undercapitalization," a singular noun, so the verb should also be singular: "is" rather than "are." (B) is incorrect because it fails to correct this error. Choice (D) is incorrect because, though it does correct the error in the original, it introduces a new error. The structure of the sentence identifies "cause" with the singular subject "undercapitalization." Finally, (E) too corrects the error, but (E) is incorrect because it changes the meaning of the original sentence. The original sentence asserts that undercapitalization is the most important of all causes of failure, but (E) says only that undercapitalization is a more important cause of failure than management errors—a considerably weaker assertion.

Not all original sentences contain an error:

Question 6-2

Most recent graduates from law school *prepare for their bar exams by listening to lectures that* are designed to review fundamental concepts of law.

(A) prepare for their bar exams by listening to lectures that
(B) prepare for his bar exam by listening to lectures that
(C) prepare for their bar exams and listen to lectures that
(D) prepare for their bar exams and listen to lectures which
(E) listen to lectures to prepare for their bar exams that

The underlined portion of the original sentence contains no error. So the correct answer is (A). (B) is incorrect because it introduces a new error. The pronoun "their" refers to "graduates," so it must be in the plural rather than the singular. Both (C) and (D) change the meaning of the original sentence, for they imply that listening to review lectures is an activity different from preparing for the exams. Finally, (E), too, changes the meaning of the original, for (E) asserts that the bar exams, rather than the lectures, are designed to review legal concepts.

It is also possible that the original sentence will contain more than one error.

164 — Be alert for sentences containing multiple errors.

Question 6-3

It was expected that the committee would recommend more stringent requirements for graduation, but its members *will make no formal report until they studied further the decline in test scores and their cause*.

(A) will make no formal report until they studied further the decline in test scores and their cause
(B) will make no formal report until it studied further the decline in test scores and their cause
(C) will make no formal report until they have further studied the test scores, their declines and their causes
(D) will make no formal report until they have studied further the decline in test scores and its cause
(E) have made no formal report until they will study further the decline in test scores and its cause

There are two errors in the original. First, there is a wrong choice of verb tense. Since the committee plans further study in the future, we must use "have studied" rather than "studied." This places the study before the act of making the formal report. Second, the pronoun "their" is intended to refer to "decline," a singular noun, so "their" also should be singular, "its." (D) corrects both errors. (B) fails to correct either error. (C) makes an attempt to correct the errors in the original, but it ends up distorting the sentence. (E) makes the second correction; but (E) not only fails to correct the problem of verb tense, it actually makes the error worse.

When an original sentence contains multiple errors, the correct choice must eliminate each of the errors. In fact, an original sentence may be so messy that it has to be completely rewritten to correct all errors:

Question 6-4

In order to assess their strengths and weaknesses and placing them in classes of appropriate levels of difficulty, on admission to the department a battery of achievement tests is given to all students.

(A) In order to assess their strengths and weaknesses and placing them in classes of appropriate levels of difficulty, on admission to the department a battery of achievement tests is given to all students.
(B) An assessment is made of each student's strengths and weaknesses to place them in classes of appropriate levels of difficulty by giving them a battery of achievement tests on admission to the department.
(C) On admission to the department, a battery of achievement tests is given to all students in order to assess their strengths and weaknesses to place them in classes of appropriate levels of difficulty.
(D) When they are admitted to the department, all students are subjected to a battery of achievement tests in order to determine his or her strengths and weaknesses preparatory to placing them in classes of appropriate levels of difficulty.
(E) On admission to the department, all students are given a battery of achievement tests to assess their strengths and weaknesses and place them in classes of appropriate levels of difficulty.

The correct answer is (E), and the sentence required considerable rewriting. In the first place, "placing" must be changed to conform it to "to assess," thereby preserving parallelism of form between those two. Second, the placement of the phrase "on admission to the department" suggests that the "battery of achievement tests," not the students, has been admitted to the department. Third, the introductory phrase "In order to assess . . . difficulty" should be closer to the main verb of the sentence "given." (E) makes the needed changes.

Choice (B) is incorrect because it fails to place the phrase "on admission to the department" so that it clearly modifies "students." (B) also introduces a new error. The pronoun "them" is intended to refer to "each student's," but the one is plural and the other singular. As it reads, (B) suggests that the strengths and weaknesses are to be placed in classes. (C) is incorrect because the placement of the introductory phrase still implies that the battery of tests has been admitted to the department. (D) at least has the merit of attempting to correct that weakness, but (D) introduces difficulties of pronoun-antecedent agreement. The sentence begins by speaking of students, in the plural, but shifts to the singular, his or her; and then returns to the plural "them."

It is possible that the entire original sentence will be underlined and yet the correct answer will be (A). Still, *Question 6-4* nicely illustrates that correcting every error may require more than just changing a verb tense here or substituting a pronoun there.

WHAT IS BEING TESTED?

According to Educational Testing Service (the test developer), sentence correction is used to test <u>*correct and effective* expression.</u> Let us discuss each of these ideas in turn.

First, as you might suspect, the notion of correct expression includes observance of the standard rules of grammar, but grammar does not define the entire scope of correct expression. To be correct, a statement must also make sense. To make the distinction, in an overly dramatic fashion, compare the following statements:

> Each student is to bring their book to school.
> This stone was dreaming of Vienna so I wrapped its nap in a paper bag.

The first statement is grammatically incorrect, but we easily perceive the meaning; and to make it grammatically correct we need only conform the pronoun "their" to the noun "student," or vice versa. The second statement is already grammatically acceptable. The subject "stone" agrees with the verb "was," and the "its" agrees in number with its antecedent, "stone," and so on. The second statement, however, makes absolutely no sense. Clear expression requires both grammatical and logical soundness.

To see the distinction between an error that might be called strictly grammatical and one that is more in the nature of an error of logic, both placed in the context of the exam, compare the following examples:

Question 6-5

The psychotherapist does not cure the patient by administering a treatment; <u>*they listen to the patient and invite*</u> the patient to treat himself.

(A) they listen to the patient and invite
(B) he listens to the patient and invites
(C) he hears the patient and invites
(D) their listening to the patient invites
(E) by listening to the patient, they invite

Question 6-6

Orlando searched every bookstore in the city for a handbook <u>*on how to prepare to take the GMAT without success*</u>.

(A) on how to prepare to take the GMAT without success
(B) on preparation to take the GMAT without success
(C) on preparing to take the GMAT without success

(D) about how to prepare to take the GMAT without success
(E) on how to prepare to take the GMAT, but his effort was not successful

Question 6-5 can be viewed as an exercise in grammar, but *Question 6-6* is more a problem of logical expression.

The correct answer to *Question 6-5* is (B). The original contains an error in grammar. The first clause uses the singular "psychotherapist," but the second clause makes a grammatically unacceptable shift to the plural. (B) corrects this by changing the plural "they" to the singular "it," and conforming the verbs. (C) is incorrect because it changes the meaning of the sentence; "hear" and "listen" do not have exactly the same meaning. (D) is incorrect for the same reason: it is not the act of listening itself that invites the patient to treat himself. Finally, (E) fails for the same reason that (D) fails.

The correct answer to *Question 6-6* is (E). The sentence, as originally constructed, seems to suggest that our would-be test taker is looking for a book in order to learn how to fail the exam: ". . . to take the GMAT *without success*." But that is not logical. The sentence contains an ambiguity that interferes with a clear statement of the intended meaning. Choice (E) corrects this by making it clear that the phrase "without success" refers to Orlando's efforts to find a book and not to his attempt to pass the GMAT. (B), (C), and (D) are incorrect because they fail to correct the original error.

We do not insist on a sharp division between questions of grammar and questions of logic. Grammar and logic are intertwined. We draw the distinction in order to make the point that sentence correction is not a grammar test, per se; but we know that the mere mention of grammar prompts some readers to dust off the old freshman composition handbook and start memorizing the forgotten rules.

Now let us turn to that other aspect of correct expression: effectiveness. Effectiveness in turn has two aspects: clarity and conciseness, and proper word choice. First, correct expression is both clear and concise; it avoids awkward sentence structures and needless repetition. Consider the following example:

Question 6-7

Most pacifists oppose all forms of organized violence *out of religious or philosophical commitment to the sanctity of human life.*

(A) out of religious or philosophical commitment to the sanctity of human life
(B) by their committing themselves religiously or philosophically to the sanctity of human life
(C) in that human life commands their religious or philosophical commitment
(D) in that they sanctify, religiously or philosophically, human life
(E) committing themselves to the sanctity of human life in their religion or philosophy

The correct answer to *Question 6-7* is (A). The sentence as originally rendered is free of grammatical errors and makes its point in a logical fashion. Each of the remaining choices suffers (at least) from the defect of awkwardness. (C) is a particularly nice example. Notice that it attempts to say only in very roundabout and stilted language what the original sentence asserts in a fairly direct fashion. Of course, you might find other things wrong with the incorrect choices, but we offer them at this point as examples of answers that are unacceptable because, if for no other reason, they are awkward.

Sentence Correction / 149

The other aspect of effective expression is word choice. Sometimes a sentence will be incorrect because the wrong word has been used or because the use of a word is not idiomatic:

Question 6-8

Many educators *sustain* <u>that high tuitions and bleak job prospects discourage many good students to enter</u> graduate school.

(A) sustain that high tuitions and bleak job prospects discourage many good students to enter
(B) sustain that high tuitions and bleak job prospects discourage many good students by entering
(C) sustain that high tuitions and bleak job prospects are discouraging many good students for entering
(D) maintain that high tuitions and bleak job prospects discourage many good students to enter
(E) maintain that high tuitions and bleak job prospects discourage many good students from entering

The correct answer is (E). There are two errors in the original. One, the word "sustain" simply does not have the meaning intended by the structure of the sentence. "Maintain," however, will do the trick. Notice that there is a similarity between the two words "sustain" and "maintain." When a question contains an error such as this, the plausibility of the original sentence is usually based on such similarity. After all, if the original sentence had used "build," "prepare," or "grate," the error would be much too obvious.

The second error is the use of "to enter," a phrase that is not idiomatic; that is, it is not acceptable in the context of this sentence. We recognize that the structure of the sentence requires "discourage . . . from entering" not "discourage . . . to enter." There is no other justification for the change. It is just that "discourage . . . to enter" does not accord with standard usage.

165 — Sentence correction tests correct (grammatical and logical) and effective (clear, concise, and idiomatic) expression.

166 — Ignore spelling and capitalization entirely.

As for punctuation, sentence correction never tests punctuation *per se*. Should answer choices differ in punctuation, this will be because they also have fundamentally different structures. The focus of the question would be some point of grammatical or logical structure, and any change in punctuation would be related to some change in the underlying wording of the sentence:

Question 6-9

Three weeks ago, while pouring the concrete, a heavy steel beam collapsed.

(A) Three weeks ago, while pouring the concrete, a heavy steel beam collapsed.
(B) While pouring the concrete, a heavy steel beam collapsed three weeks ago.
(C) Three weeks ago, a heavy steel beam collapsed while pouring the concrete.
(D) A steel beam collapsed three weeks ago while the concrete was being poured.
(E) A steel beam collapsed by pouring the concrete three weeks ago.

The correct answer is (D). The error in the original is a matter of logical structure. It seems as though the heavy steel beam was doing the pouring, but that cannot be the intended meaning of the sentence. (D) correctly states the intended meaning by relocating the modifying phrases, but that requires changes in punctuation. Whereas the original sentence uses two commas, (D) uses no commas; but the changes in (D) are justified by considerations of meaning, not punctuation. Similarly, the remaining choices are incorrect because they fail to relocate the modifying phrases, not because they use incorrect punctuation. In fact, each of the other choices, though incorrect as a matter of sentence structure, is punctuated correctly. Thus:

167 Assume that all answer choices are correctly punctuated.

ABOUT SENTENCE CORRECTION SECTIONS

First, you will find 25 questions which must be answered in the 30-minute time limit. Second, the questions will seem to become more difficult as you advance through the section. Third, there is a great deal of reading to be done in the sentence correction section. The section is not just a matter of 25 simple sentences. Some of the originals are quite long, and each original is followed by four different ways of trying to say the same thing. Further, more than one choice for a question, perhaps even all, will seem to have merit. Therefore, this section requires considerable thought.

Pacing is as important in sentence correction as in math or reading. More is required than just reading a sentence and circling an error. Not only must you find the error, you must also select the best way of rewriting the sentence. There is no formula by which you can determine how quickly you must move. If all questions were of an equal level of difficulty, you could divide 30 minutes by 25 questions and conclude that you have, on the average, 1.2 minutes to spend on each question. Since the questions are not all of the same level of difficulty, however, you must devote less than this to the first questions so that you have some extra time for the difficult questions.

COMMON PATTERNS OF SENTENCE CORRECTION

Five Common Grammatical Errors

1. One common grammatical error that is tested with some degree of frequency is lack of agreement between subject and verb. In its simplest form, this is usually highly evident:

> The books is on the shelf. (Error!)
> The teacher admonish the class to calm down. (Error!)

Of course, you should not expect to encounter such obvious examples on the test. There are three techniques the test writers have used in the past to obscure the connection between subject and verb.

> **168** When checking for agreement between the subject and verb, (1) ignore intervening words between the subject and verb; (2) treat compound subjects as plural; and (3) be alert for sentences in which the verb precedes the subject.

The first technique used to obscure the connection between the subject and the verb is the insertion of material between the two. If you are not careful, by the time you reach the verb, you will have forgotten the subject and will have no way of knowing whether the verb does or does not agree with the subject. Consider the following examples:

> Star performers in the movies or on television usually earns substantial income from royalties.
>
> One school of thought maintains that the federal deficit, not exorbitant corporate profits and excessively high wages, cause most of the inflation we are now experiencing.
>
> A recent survey shows that a household in which both the wife and the husband are pursuing careers stand a better chance of surviving intact than one in which only the husband works.

In each of these three sentences there is a failure of agreement between subject and verb:

> performers ... earns (Error!)
> deficit ... cause (Error!)
> household ... stand (Error!)

The error may not be immediately evident, however, because of the intervening material. In the first sentence the subject is separated from the verb by prepositional phrases. In the second, the subject and verb are separated by a parenthetical expression. In the third, a clause intervenes between the subject and verb.

The plausibility of the incorrect verb choice, and therefore the chance that the error will go unnoticed, is strengthened by placing a word or phrase near the verb that might be mistaken for the subject:

> television ... earns
> profits and wages ... cause
> careers ... stand

If the first word of each of the pairs had been the subject, then there would have been no failure of agreement.

A second problem of agreement to be alert for involves the use of a compound subject. Usually when the subject of a sentence consists of two or more elements joined by the conjunction "and," the subject is considered plural and requires a plural verb:

> Of the seven candidates, only John, Bill, and he was past office holders. (Error!)

The subject, "John, Bill, and he," is compound (joined by "and") and requires a plural verb—even though "he" itself is singular.

Be careful not to confuse the compound subject with the disjunctive subject. When elements of the subject are joined by "or," the verb must agree with the element nearest to it:

> Of the seven candidates, John, Bill, or he is likely to win.

In this case, the elements are joined by "or," so the verb must agree with "he."

Finally, you should be alert for inverted sentence structures, those in which the verb precedes the subject:

> Although the first amendment to the Constitution does guarantee freedom of speech, the Supreme Court has long recognized that there has to be some restrictions on the exercise of this right.
>
> Jennifer must have been doubly pleased that day, for seated in the gallery to watch her receive the award was her brother, her parents, and her husband.

In both of these sentences we have a failure of agreement between subject and verb. Here the relationship is obscured by the order in which the elements appear in the sentence: verb comes before subject:

(there) has . . . restrictions (Error!)
was her brother, her parents, and her husband. (Error!)

You should, then, pay careful attention to the connection between subject and verb, no matter how those elements are presented. You may even need to isolate each element to make sure that the needed agreement is there:

Question 6-10

Diplomats sent to an unstable region or a genuinely hostile territory usually *is assigned an aide or chauffeur who function* also as a body guard.

(A) is assigned an aide or chauffeur who function
(B) are assigned an aide or chauffeur who function
(C) are assigned an aide or chauffeur who functions
(D) is assigned an aide or chauffeur that function
(E) are assigned an aide or chauffeur which functions

There are two errors in the original sentence, both failure of agreement between subject and verb:

Diplomats . . . is assigned (Error!)
aide or chauffeur (who) function (Error!)

The correct answer is (C). (C) eliminates the first error by changing the singular verb, "is assigned," to the plural, thereby making it conform to the plural subject, "Diplomats." (C) also corrects the second error. The pronoun "who," which is the subject of the modifying clause, takes its number from its antecedent. Since "who" replaces "aide or chauffeur," the verb must agree with "aide or chauffeur." As we noted above, a disjunctive subject needs a verb that agrees with the element closest to the verb. In this case, the element closest to the verb is "chauffeur," and as your ear will tell you, the correct verb would be "functions": chauffeur functions.

2. A second important pattern in the sentence correction section is the use of pronouns. We may summarize the rules for correct pronoun usage in our next key:

> **169** A pronoun (1) must have an antecedent (referent) to which it (2) refers clearly and with which it (3) agrees.

First, a pronoun is used as a substitute for a noun. The noun it replaces is called its antecedent or its referent. With the exception of certain idioms such as "*It* is raining," a pronoun that does not have an antecedent is used incorrectly:

Although Glen is president of the student body, he has not yet passed his English exam, and because of it, he will not graduate with the rest of his class.

The damage done by Senator Smith's opposition to the policy of equal employment is undeniable, but that is exactly what he attempted to do in his speech Thursday.

In the first sentence, what is the antecedent of "it?" Do not respond, "he has not yet passed his English exam," for that is a complete thought (clause) and not just a noun. "It" is not a pronoun substitute for that entire thought. You would do better by responding that "it" refers to Glen's *failure* to pass the exam, for at least "it" would then have an antecedent. This move fails, however, because "failure" does not appear in noun form in the sentence. In other words, the "it" "wants" to refer to a noun, but there is no noun to function as its point of reference. The sentence must be rewritten: "because of that fact, he will not graduate...."

In the second sentence, "that" functions as a relative pronoun—it relates something in the first clause to the second clause. But to what does "that" refer? When you think you have found it, test your possibility by substituting it for "that" in the second clause. After all, if the sentence makes sense using the pronoun "that," it should also make sense when you substitute the pronoun's antecedent for the pronoun. Is the antecedent "damage?" This attempt fails:

> but "the damage" is exactly what he attempted to do....

Perhaps, then, the antecedent is "opposition" or "undeniable":

> but the "opposition" is exactly what he attempted to do....
> but the "undeniable" is exactly what he attempted to do....

There are no other candidates for antecedent, so we must conclude that the use of "that" is incorrect. We could rewrite the sentence: "but he did attempt to deny...."

Second, the antecedent of the pronoun must be clear from the structure of the sentence:

> Edward's father died before he reached his 20th birthday, so he never finished his education.
>
> In 1980, the University Council voted to rescind provision 3 which made it easier for some students to graduate.

In the first sentence, it is not clear whether the father died before he reached the age of 20 or before Edward reached the age of 20. Further, it is not entirely clear whose education remained unfinished. Similarly, in the second sentence the antecedent of "which" is not made clear. It may refer to the provision or it may refer to the Council's action. Both sentences would have to be rewritten to make clear the antecedents of the pronouns, and on the actual exam, the structure of the question (the available choices), would guide you in determining which of two arguably correct meanings was intended by the original sentence.

The third requirement is that the pronoun agree with its antecedent. For example, if the antecedent is singular, then the pronoun must be singular. Consider the following sentences:

> Historically, the dean of a college was also a professor, but today they are usually professional administrators.
>
> The male lion, the epitome of strength and bravery, is actually very lazy; they are content to let the lioness do their hunting for them.

In the first sentence, "they" must refer to "dean," but "dean" is singular and "they" is plural, an error. The sentence can be corrected in either of two ways. It can be corrected by changing the first clause to the plural:

> Historically, college deans were also professors, ...

or by changing the second clause to the singular:

> . . . he is usually a professional administrator.

or perhaps even better:

> . . . the dean is usually a professor administrator.

In the second sentence, "lion" is the antecedent for three pronouns in the second clause, "they," "their," and "them." But "lion" is singular and the pronouns are plural, an error. Again the correction could proceed from either direction:

> Male lions . . . are actually very lazy; . . .

or

> . . . he is content to let the lioness do his hunting for him.

Of course, the exam format would allow you no choice in the matter. Only one correct option would be available, and the usual format is to require that you change the pronouns. We point out, as a reminder, that the correct choice would conform all pronouns and would make the appropriate adjustments to verbs as well:

Question 6-11

The male lion, the epitome of strength and bravery, is actually very lazy; <u>they are content to let the lioness do their hunting for them.</u>

(A) they are content to let the lioness do their hunting for them
(B) they are content to let the lionesses do their hunting for them
(C) he is content to let the lioness do their hunting for him
(D) he is content to let the lioness do his hunting for him
(E) he is content to let the lioness do her hunting for them

The correct answer, (D), not only changes all three pronouns to the singular, it changes the verb to the singular as well. (B) is incorrect because it makes none of the needed changes. (C) is incorrect because it fails to correct the second pronoun. Finally, (E) is incorrect because it changes the meaning of the original sentence.

3. Faulty parallelism is a grammatical error that appears frequently on the test.

> **170** Whenever elements of a sentence perform similar or equal functions, they should have the same form.

Consider the following sentences:

> At most colleges, the dominant attitude among students is that gaining admission to professional graduate school is more important than to obtain a well-rounded education.
>
> To demand that additional seasonings be placed on the table is insulting the chef's judgment on the proper balance of ingredients.
>
> The review was very critical of the film, citing the poor photography, the weak plot, and the dialogue was stilted.

Each sentence contains an error of parallelism.

In the first sentence, "gaining admission" and "to obtain" must both have the same form. Either both must be in the infinitive form or both must be in the gerund form; for example, "gaining admission . . . is more important than obtaining. . . ." In the second sentence, the subject, "to demand," and the predicate complement, "insulting," must both have the same form: "To demand . . . is to insult. . . ." In the third sentence each element in the series of bad features should have the same form: "the photography was poor, the plot was weak, and the dialogue was stilted." Or the third sentence might be used as a test question in the following way:

Question 6-12

> The review was very critical of the film, citing the poor photography, the weak plot, *and the dialogue was stilted.*
>
> (A) and the dialogue was stilted
> (B) but the dialogue was stilted
> (C) while the dialogue was stilted
> (D) and the stilted dialogue
> (E) and also including the stilted dialogue

The correct answer to this question would be (D), for (D) correctly conforms the clause (". . . and the dialogue was stilted.") to the noun form of the other elements. (B) and (C) are incorrect because they fail to correct the faulty parallelism. (E) is incorrect, for while (E) makes the needed change, it introduces unnecessary verbiage, making the sentence too wordy.

4. A fourth group of grammatical errors involves split construction. We use the term "split construction" to refer to phrases in which a thought is interrupted by intervening material to be completed later in the sentence:

> The officials were not only aware of but actually encouraged the misreporting of scores.

This sentence uses a perfectly acceptable split construction. Ordinarily, the object of a preposition closely follows the preposition: ". . . aware of the misreporting." Here, the object of the preposition is separated from the preposition by the material "but actually encouraged." This is unobjectionable as long as the thought is properly completed. There is a danger, however, that the intervening material will throw something off:

171 — Make sure that split constructions are properly completed.

Consider the following faulty sentences:

> Opponents of the President's foreign policy disclosed yesterday that the CIA not only knew but tacitly encouraged terrorist activities in Central America.

> Her colleagues always speak of Professor Collins as a person who has and will always be sensitive to the needs of younger students.

> Judging from the pricing policies of many large corporations, maintaining a stable share of the market is as important, if not more important than, making a large profit.

In each of these sentences there is an error of split construction. There is a missing preposition in the first sentence. The CIA did not know the terrorist activities, rather it knew *of* the activities. In the second sentence, the error is in the verb. The auxiliary verb "has" needs the verb "been," but "been" does not appear in the sentence. The sentence could be corrected by completing the construction: ". . . has been and will always be. . . ." In the third sentence, the error is an incomplete comparison. The sentence should read ". . . as important *as*, if not more important than. . . ."

It is the intervening material that makes these errors difficult to spot. (Compare intervening material between the subject and the verb.) So you must always check to make sure that a split construction has been properly completed:

Question 6-13

An objective reporter, Holmes has spared <u>neither criticism nor praise for</u> the Mayor's programs.

(A) neither criticism nor praise for
(B) either criticism or praise for
(C) neither criticism of nor praise for
(D) either criticism of or praise for
(E) both criticism of and praise for

The correct answer is (C). The original sentence uses a split construction which is not complete. "Criticism" requires the preposition "of," "criticism" cannot use the preposition "for." (B) fails to make the correction, and (D), though it makes the correction, introduces a new error, by making the sentence ambiguous. (E) is incorrect because it changes the meaning of the original sentence.

5. The final grammatical error to be alert for is failure to use a noun clause where one is required:

> Why American car manufacturers did not reduce the size of their cars earlier than they did is a mystery to most market experts.

> The reason the saxophone is a popular jazz instrument is because the timbre of the saxophone can approximate that of the human voice.

The error in the first sentence is "why," and the error in the second sentence is "because." In both sentences, a noun clause is required, so "that" should have been used in both cases:

> **172** — "Because" and "why" cannot start noun clauses.

Consider the following example:

Question 6-14

<u>The reason the manager changed catchers was because</u> he hoped that the opposing side would put in a left-handed pitcher.

(A) The reason the manager changed catchers was because
(B) The reason that catchers were changed by the manager was because
(C) The reason the manager changed catchers which
(D) The manager changed catchers because
(E) The manager changed catchers, the reason being

The original sentence makes the error of using "because" to introduce a noun clause. (D) corrects the error by eliminating the need for a separate noun clause. (B) not only fails to correct the error, it introduces additional awkwardness into the sentence. (C) introduces a new error as well, for with (C), the sentence would have no main verb at all. Finally, (E) makes the attempt to correct the error, but (E) fails because it uses the unacceptable phrase "the reason being" instead of the simple and more direct "because."

Five Common Problems of Logical Expression

1. One problem of logical expression that appears on almost every exam is faulty or illogical comparison, that is, the attempt to compare two things that cannot logically be compared:

> Today, life expectancies of both men and women are much higher compared to the turn of the century when living conditions were much harsher.

> The average salary of a professional basketball player is higher than the top-level management of most corporations.

A comparison can only be made between like items. Yet, in the first sentence we see an attempt to compare life expectancies with "the turn of the century." Those are two dissimilar concepts. The sentence could be corrected by simply adding the phrase "those of." Now we have life expectancies compared to life expectancies, and that is a logical comparison. We find the same error in the second sentence. There, an attempt is made to compare average salary to management. The error can be corrected in the same way: ". . . is higher than those of the top-level management. . . ."

> **173** Be alert for sentences which attempt to make an illogical comparison between two dissimilar items.

This is illustrated by the following example:

Question 6-15

<u>Like Neil Simon, many of Tennessee Williams's plays</u> reflect a culture familiar to the playwright.

- (A) LIke Neil Simon, many of Tennessee Williams's plays
- (B) Many of Tennessee Williams's plays, like Neil Simon's
- (C) Many of Tennessee Williams's plays, like Neil Simon
- (D) Many of Neil Simon and Tennessee Williams's plays
- (E) As with the plays of Neil Simon, many of Tennessee Williams's plays

The correct answer is (B). The sentence is guilty of illogical comparison; it attempts to compare Neil Simon with the plays of Tennessee Williams. (B) corrects the error by making it clear that plays are to be compared with plays, not plays with playwright. (C) is incorrect because it fails to correct the error; (C) still attempts to compare Neil Simon with the plays of Tennessee Williams. (D) can be eliminated because it changes the meaning of the original sentence, suggesting that Simon and Williams coauthored the plays. Finally, (E) is incorrect because it corrects the error only at the expense of clarity and directness.

2. A second fairly common problem of logical expression is poor choice of verb tense:

> **174** Make sure that verb tenses properly reflect the order and duration of action described.

An error in choice of verb tense appears in each of the following sentences:

> As soon as Linda finished writing her dissertation, she will take a well-earned vacation in Paris.

> A recent study shows that many mothers reenter the labor force after their children left home.

In the first sentence, both the writing and the vacation must be placed in the same time frame. As written, the sentence places the two actions in different, unconnected time frames. Depending on whether Linda has already completed the dissertation (an issue that would be settled by the question format on the exam), the sentence could be corrected in either of two ways:

> As soon as Linda finishes writing her dissertation, she will take a well-earned vacation in Paris.
>
> or
>
> As soon as Linda finished writing her dissertation, she took a well-earned vacation in Paris.

The first sentence states that both events have not yet occurred and that the writing will precede vacation. The second sentence states that the events are completed, and that the writing preceded the vacation.

In the second sentence, the verb "left" is incorrect. The verb "reenter" is describing a present, ongoing action. The sentence can be corrected by making it clear that children leaving home is also a present phenomenon:

> A recent study shows that many mothers reenter the labor force after their children leave home.
>
> or
>
> A recent study shows that many mothers reenter the labor force after their children have left home.

Either sentence is acceptable since both make it clear that the leaving home is not a completed past action but an ongoing phenomenon.

Now consider an example presented in exam format:

Question 6-16

The producers realized the concert *has been a success as they heard* the cheers and applause of the audience.

(A) has been a success as they heard
(B) has been a success hearing
(C) was a success hearing
(D) had been a success when they heard
(E) succeeded in that they heard

The correct answer is (D). The logic of the sentence requires that the concert be a completed act occurring before the realization of the producers, but the original choice of "has been a success" implies an ongoing action, not a complete action. (B) fails to make this needed correction. (C) does make a possible correction, as it implies that the concert was over when the producers realized that it was a success; but (C) introduces a new error, the awkward "hearing." (E) too attempts to make the correction, but the result is needlessly wordy and awkward. Finally, (D) makes not only the change in verb tense, (D) changes "as" to "when," indicating that the hearing of the cheers and applause preceded the realization of the producers.

3. A third error of logical expression, and one which appears on virtually every exam and on some exams more than once, is the infamous misplaced modifier:

175 — Be alert for sentences with ambiguous or incorrect modification.

Generally, a modifier should be placed as close to what it modifies as possible. A modifier which is too far from what it is intended to modify or too close to some other important element will seem to modify the wrong part of the sentence:

> Stuffed with herb dressing, trussed neatly, and baked to a golden hue, Aunt Fannie proudly served her famous holiday turkey.

> The doctor said gently to the patient that there was nothing wrong with a smile.

> At the tailgate party, Fred served cold beer to his thirsty guests in paper cups.

As for the first sentence, poor Aunt Fannie! The proximity of the introductory modifier to Aunt Fannie, the next main element of the sentence, suggests that Aunt Fannie was stuffed, trussed, and baked. The sentence can be corrected by relocating the modifying phrase:

> Aunt Fannie proudly served her famous holiday turkey, stuffed with herb dressing, trussed neatly, and baked to a golden hue.

or by rewriting the sentence as follows:

> Stuffed with herb dressing, trussed neatly, and baked to a golden hue, the famous holiday turkey was proudly served by Aunt Fannie.

The second sentence is ambiguous and could mean either that there is nothing wrong with smiling or that the doctor said with a smile that nothing was wrong with the patient. Finally, in the third sentence, the location of the prepositional phrase "in paper cups" implies that it is the guests who are in the paper cups, not the beer. The sentence can be corrected by repositioning the modifying phrase so that it is closer to what it is intended to modify:

> At the tailgate party, Fred served cold beer in paper cups to his thirsty guests.

Of course, the available choices will limit you in making the sentence correct:

Question 6-17

At the height of the victory celebration, Neimann sketched the winning jockey waving to a crowd of enthusiastic fans with pen and ink.

(A) At the height of the victory celebration, Neimann sketched the winning jockey waving to a crowd of enthusiastic fans with pen and ink.
(B) Using pen and ink at the height of the victory celebration, Neimann sketched the winning jockey waving to a crowd of enthusiastic fans.
(C) At the height of the victory celebration and with a pen and ink, Neimann

sketched the winning jockey waving to a crowd of enthusiastic fans.
(D) Using pen and ink, Neimann sketched the winning jockey waving to a crowd of enthusiastic fans at the height of the victory celebration.
(E) At the height of the victory celebration, the winning jockey waving to a crowd of enthusiastic fans was sketched by Neimann with pen and ink.

The difficulty with the original sentence is placement of the modifiers. The sentence asserts either that the winning jockey was waving to the fans who had pen and ink or that the winning jockey used the pen and ink to wave to the fans; both nonsensical interpretations. The intended meaning of the sentence is that the sketch was executed using pen and ink. (D) makes this clear and is the correct answer. (B) attempts to make the correction but fails because it leaves an ambiguity in the sentence. Because of the phrase "at the height...," is close to "pen and ink," "at the height...," appears to modify "pen and ink," but "at the height" is intended to refer to the jockey's waving. (C) fails for the same reason. (E) can be eliminated because it uses the awkward passive voice.

4. A fourth type of error of logical expression is ambiguity in scope. This occurs when there is no clear division between two ideas, so that the ideas seem to merge:

> After the arrest, the accused was charged with resisting arrest and criminal fraud.
>
> The recent changes in the tax law will affect primarily workers who wait tables in restaurants, operate concessions in public places, and drive taxis.

In the first sentence, the scope of "resisting" is not clear. The sentence can be read to assert that the accused was charged with resisting criminal fraud. The intended scope can be made clear by inserting a "with": "...charged with resisting arrest and *with* criminal fraud." This clearly indicates that there are two separate ideas, not one. In the second sentence, the use of "and" seems to tie three separate ideas together; that is, it is those workers who do all three jobs who will be affected. That clearly is not the intent of the sentence. That these are three separate ideas can be made clear by changing "and" to "or," or by making a series of parallel ideas: "...workers who wait tables in restaurants, workers who operate concessions in public places, and workers who drive taxis."

176 — Be alert for sentences that run two or more ideas together.

Question 6-18

<u>Along with an end to feather-bedding and no-show jobs,</u> the new head of the Transit Authority has eliminated many other inefficient employment practices.

(A) Along with an end to feather-bedding and no-show jobs,
(B) In addition to eliminating feather-bedding and no-show jobs,
(C) Not only did he end feather-bedding and no-show jobs, but
(D) Besides feather-bedding and no-show jobs coming to an end,
(E) Together with the ending of feather-bedding and no-show jobs,

The original sentence has the structure: "Along with an end . . . , the new head has eliminated. . . ." This suggests that the new head of the Transit Authority has eliminated the end to feather-bedding and no shows. The sentence can be corrected by making it clear that the end of feather-bedding and no-show jobs does not come within the scope of "eliminated." (B), the correct answer, accomplishes this. (C), (D), and (E) are all incorrect because they are awkward.

5. A fifth category of problems of logical expression is the miscellaneous category. A sentence will intend to say one thing but actually say another:

> The last time the football team finished with a winning record was Coach Bob Johnson.
>
> A childless charwoman's daughter, Dr. Roberts was a self-made woman.
>
> If the present interest rates fall drastically, the dollar will lose much of its value on the foreign exchange.

Each of these sentences may seem, on its face, plausible, but a closer reading will show that each one contains an error of logical expression. As for the first, there it is asserted that "The last time . . . was Coach Bob Johnson." Coach Johnson is not a point in time. The sentence intended to say "The last time . . . was during Coach Bob Johnson's tenure," or something like that. The second sentence is actually self-contradictory. As written, it asserts that Dr. Roberts was the daughter of a childless charwoman. In that case, Dr. Roberts would indeed have been a self-made woman! What the sentence intends to say about Dr. Roberts is that she was both childless and the daughter of a charwoman. Finally, the third sentence is a bit more subtle. It suggests that present interest rates can change, but that is internally inconsistent, for if the interest rate changes, the result is a new interest rate—not a changed "present" rate. The sentence can easily be corrected by deleting the word "present." We refer to these errors as miscellaneous errors, for there are as many possible examples as there are possible errors in human reasoning. In an attempt to make some generalization regarding them, we add the key:

177 — Determine whether the logical structure of the sentence asserts what the sentence intends to say.

Consider the following example:

Question 6-19

Mary Lou was awarded the gold medal because she scored *more points than any child participating* in the field day.

(A) more points than any child participating
(B) more points than any other child participating
(C) most points than any child participating
(D) more points than any child who had participated
(E) more points as any child participating

The correct answer to this example is (B). The original sentence is logically contradictory because it asserts that Mary Lou scored more points than anyone—even herself! The sentence intends to say that Mary Lou scored more points than anyone *else* did, and (B) makes this needed correction.

Clarity, Conciseness, and Word Choice

The possibilities for error in these categories are too numerous to admit of classification. Instead, we will illustrate each type of error with one or two examples.

1. Sometimes a sentence will be grammatically and logically correct and yet be in need of correction because it is awkward:

> The giant condor is able to spread its wings up to 25 feet. (Poor)
>
> The giant condor has a wingspread of up to 25 feet. (Better)
>
> Although most students would benefit from further study of the sciences, doing so is frightening to most of them in that science courses are more difficult than liberal arts courses. (Poor)
>
> Although most students would benefit from further study of the sciences, most of them are afraid to take such courses because they are more difficult than liberal arts courses. (Better)
>
> Given that the Incas lacked the wheel, the buildings at Machu Picchu are more astonishing than any Greek temples that are comparable as an achievement. (Poor)
>
> Given that the Incas lacked the wheel, the buildings at Machu Picchu are more astonishing than any comparable Greek temple. (Better)

In each case, the second sentence more clearly and less awkwardly renders the thought:

> **178** Prefer an answer choice that renders the thought more directly and less awkwardly.

This key is likely to be particularly helpful in eliminating answer choices, for many choices (as opposed to original sentences) are wrong because they are awkward. In particular:

> **179** Look with disfavor upon a construction using "being" or the passive voice.

Keep in mind that the test writer must offer not only an acceptable sentence as the correct choice, but must also include four unacceptable choices. A favorite way of writing an unacceptable choice is to include a construction using "being":

> The unemployment rate being 4 percent, there are approximately as many open jobs as there are job seekers. (Awkward)

> When the unemployment rate is 4 percent, there are approximately as many open jobs as there are job seekers. (Better)

> Resident aliens, unlike citizens, being unable to vote, have little voice in American politics. (Awkward)

> Because resident aliens, unlike citizens, are not able to vote, they have little voice in American politics. (Better)

A related move is to include a choice with an awkward use of the passive voice:

> One-fourth of the market was captured by the new computer firm. (Awkward)

> The new computer firm captured one-fourth of the market. (Better)

Question 6-20

> The sheriff called off the search for the escaped convict because he doubted that *the convict can successfully cross the river because the current was so swift.*
> (A) the convict can successfully cross the river because the current was so swift
> (B) the convict successfully crossed the river because the current was so swift
> (C) the convict successfully crossed the river being that the current was so swift
> (D) the convict would have been successful in crossing the river, the current being so swift
> (E) a successful attempt to cross the river was made by the convict because the current was so swift

The correct answer is (B), because (B) makes it clear that any attempt to cross was in the past, conforming the tense to "was so swift." (C), (D), and (E) can be eliminated because they make the sentence awkward.

2. Occasionally, an original sentence will be incorrect because it is needlessly wordy:

> The protracted discussion over which route to take continued for a long time. (Wordy)

> The discussion over which route to take continued for a long time. (Better)

> A principle aim of the proposal is chiefly to ensure and guarantee the academic freedom of students. (Wordy)

> A principle aim of the proposal is to guarantee the academic freedom of students. (Better)

To be protracted is to be continued over a long period; to be a principle aim is to be a chief aim, and to ensure is to guarantee. So each original is needlessly wordy:

166 / *101 Tips for Scoring High on the GMAT*

180 Avoid needless repetition by selecting a choice that renders the thought most concisely.

Question 6-21

For many years, jogging was was ridiculed by many people as an activity of fanatics, <u>but *however it is now growing rapidly in national popularity all across the country.*</u>

(A) however it is now growing rapidly in national popularity all across the country
(B) however it is now growing rapidly in national popularity
(C) it is now growing rapidly in national popularity across the country
(D) it is now growing rapidly in national popularity
(E) its national popularity is now increasing all across the country

The correct answer is (D). The "however" is needlessly repetitious of "but" and "all across the country" is needlessly repetitious of "national." Only (D) eliminates both problems.

3. Sometimes a sentence will be incorrect because a word is used incorrectly. This occurs when a construction is simply not idiomatic, that is, the phrase is not acceptable according to standard usage:

> The techniques of empirical observation in the social sciences are different than those in the physical sciences. (Incorrect)

> The techniques of empirical observation in the social sciences are different from those in the physical sciences. (Better)

A variation on this theme uses pairs of words that are often incorrectly used:

> John expressed his intention to make the trip, but whether ~~if~~ he will actually go is doubtful.

> Social science differs from physical science because social events are ~~not able to be measured~~ not capable of measurement.

> Herbert divided the cake ~~among~~ between Mary and Sally.

> Herbert divided the cake ~~between~~ among Mary, Sally, and himself.

> The ~~amount~~ number of students in the class declined as the semester progressed.

> There are ~~less~~ fewer students in Professor Smith's class than there are in Professor Jones's class.

Finally, the exam writer occasionally plays on the confusion between two words that sound somewhat alike, but have different meanings:

Although Bob did a good job, his position in the firm is ~~insecure~~ not secure.

The Secretary of Defense was adamantly opposed to any ~~deduction~~ reduction in the defense budget.

Before ~~dissembling~~ disassembling the scaffolding, the workers took their lunch break.

It is an ~~allusion~~ illusion that the moon is larger than Venus.

181 — Be alert for inappropriate word choice including nonidiomatic usage, commonly misused words, and words of similar sound but different meaning.

SENTENCE CORRECTION ATTACK STRATEGY

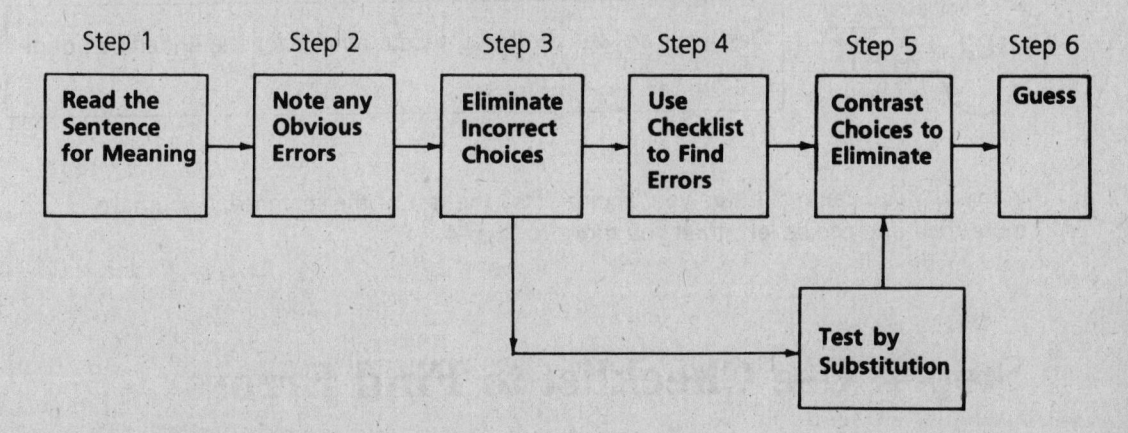

Step 1	Step 2	Step 3	Step 4	Step 5	Step 6
Read the Sentence for Meaning	Note any Obvious Errors	Eliminate Incorrect Choices	Use Checklist to Find Errors	Contrast Choices to Eliminate	Guess

Test by Substitution

The preceding flow-chart explains the steps you should take in attacking a sentence correction item.

Step 1: Read the Sentence for Meaning

The first step is simply to read the entire sentence through for meaning. After all, you cannot possibly hope to determine whether the sentence correctly expresses its intended meaning until you first learn what it intends to say.

Step 2: Note Any Obvious Errors

Go back through the sentence, reading more carefully, and note any obvious errors. Remember to be alert for the possibility of multiple errors.

Step 3: Eliminate Incorrect Choices

Remember that a choice may be incorrect because it:

1. fails to correct all of the errors in the original,
2. introduces some new error, or
3. changes the intended meaning of the original.

At this point, you will be faced with one of two situations. Either you will have eliminated all choices but one, or you will have more than one choice remaining. If you have eliminated all choices but one, test your choice by substituting for the underlined original:

> **182** Test your answer choice by substituting it for the underlined original.

In this way you can make sure your choice "fits" the rest of the sentence. If you have more than one choice left, then you move to Step 4.

Step 4: Use Checklist to Find Errors

If you are unable to eliminate all but one choice as a result of obvious errors, then you should mentally run down the checklist of errors we have presented (Keys

168–181). Of course, the relevance of any key depends on what part of the sentence has been underlined. Obviously, you do not need to ask about the agreement of subject and verb if neither the subject nor the verb is part of the underlined sentence:

> **183** Ignore any "errors" that cannot be corrected by selecting an appropriate answer choice.

You may find a construction or choice of words that you think is not entirely correct, either in the underlined portion of the sentence or in the nonunderlined portion of the sentence; yet, there may be no choice that makes the correction as needed. In that event, you just ignore the seeming error.

Question 6-22

The committee were detained in the Senate Building under an executive order *vague in its wording and admitting* of considerable debate as to its meaning.

(A) vague in its wording and admitting
(B) which wording was vague and admitted
(C) that wording was vague and admitted
(D) worded vaguely and admittedly
(E) vaguely wording and admitting

The correct answer is (A). First, you may find the construction "admitting of" a bit awkward, and given the opportunity, you would be likely to substitute some other, more familiar phrase such as "open to." In point of fact, the phrase is acceptable even if somewhat unusual. Be that as it may, even if you are of the opinion that the locution is incorrect, you are stuck with it. Choice (D) is the only choice that attempts to change the construction, and it fails miserably. Since no answer choice will correct the seeming error, you must treat it as though it is no error at all.

Similarly, many people will find an error in the construction "committee were." Again, the phrase is actually correct, though somewhat odd. "Committee" can be used as a plural noun to refer to each and every member of the group as well as a singular noun to refer to the group as whole. In any event, no answer choice touches on the issue of the agreement of subject and verb, so you treat the seeming error as no error.

On the other hand, since some errors can be corrected in more than one way, the location of the error may not be entirely in the underlined portion of the original:

Question 6-23

It seems that each generation must declare its independence from the preceding generation; and clothing, such as the beads of the sixties and the unisex fashions of the seventies, *are important symbols* of this declaration.

(A) are important symbols
(B) are highly symbolic
(C) is an important symbol

(D) is the symbol
(E) were important symbols

The correct answer is (C), and the error in the original is a failure of agreement between the singular subject "clothing" and the plural phrase "are important symbols." If you were actually composing this sentence yourself, you might correct the error in several different ways. You could change "clothing" to "clothes." Here you do not have that option, so you must select (C).

The interesting thing about *Question 6-24* is that the location of the error was not necessarily in the underlined part of the sentence. Rather, it resided in the interaction between two parts, the subject and the verb:

> **184** Be alert for possible errors that are not contained entirely in the underlined part of the sentence but result from the interaction of the underlined and the nonunderlined parts of the sentence.

Step 5: Contrast Choices to Eliminate

If at this stage you still have more than one seemingly correct possibility, you can get further leverage on the question by contrasting answer choices. It is, after all, characteristic of the exam that one of the five choices is correct. You only need to find it. So you carry forward the attack by looking at the remaining choices and consciously asking what difference does the difference make? Consider the following example:

Question 6-24

The financial consequences of the President's decision to raise tuition <u>appear at least equal, if not outweigh,</u> the academic implications of the increase.

(A) appear at least equal, if not outweigh
(B) appear at least equal to, if not outweigh
(C) appear at least equal to, if not outweighing
(D) appear at least to equal, if not to outweigh
(E) appears equal, at least, if not to outweigh

(E) is different from the other choices in using "appears" rather than "appear," but the subject of the sentence is "consequences," a plural noun, so the verb should be "appear," not "appears." This contrast allows us to eliminate (E) as incorrect.

Next, (B), (C), and (D) all include "to," a word that is lacking in the original, but the original split construction "appear at least equal . . . the academic implications" is not complete without "to." So we eliminate (A). Finally, (D) includes a second "to" before "outweigh," but (B) and (C) do not have this. What is the significance of the difference? Without the second "to," the phrase "if not outweigh" is not completed and is not parallel, so (B) and (C) are incorrect, leaving (D) as the correct choice.

When you have reached this stage, there are three further points to keep in mind. First,

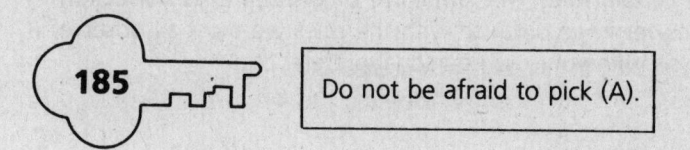

KEY 185: Do not be afraid to pick (A).

Many test takers are reluctant to pick choice (A) (signifying that the original is correct), reasoning that even though they do not see an error there, the sentence must surely be wrong because this is the sentence correction section. They conclude, therefore, they just do not know enough about grammar and expression to find the error and select one of the (B) through (E) alternatives. You must remember, however, that the answer choices are fairly randomly distributed across the five lettered categories. Although it is unlikely that there will be exactly five (A)s, five (B)s, five (C)s, five (D)s, and five (E)s, the actual distribution on any test will not deviate far from that distribution. Consequently, you can expect to find somewhere around five choice (A)s in a sentence correction section. In other words, somewhere around 5 of the 25 originals will be correct.

Second, in contrasting choices to one another for the purpose of elimination:

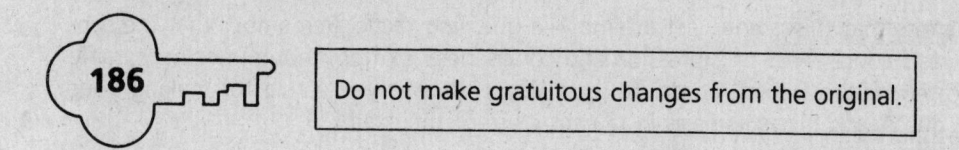

KEY 186: Do not make gratuitous changes from the original.

Do not make a change from the original unless you have a reason to make such a change. This does not mean, of course, that you must be able to formulate a fancy justification in technical terminology, but a change is not warranted unless you can explain to yourself, even if only by analogy, the reason for the change.

There is one final note to be added to this train of thought:

KEY 187: The correct response may not represent the perfect or even only correct way of rendering the sentence.

The instructions to the sentence correction section implicitly acknowledge this when they speak of finding the choice that is "better" than the other choices. "Better," after all, is a term of comparison. The correct answer is not likely to be the one, single, uniquely correct way of writing the sentence. You are likely to have your own stylistic preferences which are inconsistent with the correct response. Still, the correct answer stands as correct because, all things considered, it is the best of the five choices available.

If you find yourself objecting under your breath "Yes, but even this could be improved," or "I would have used a different word altogether," remind yourself of this last Key. So long as you recognize the intended correct answer as the choice you must make, you have done all that is required of you. It is a waste of time and intellectual effort to go further and detail the stylistic shortcomings of the test writers.

In short, writing styles are highly idiosyncratic; yet for all the great variety we find, good writing must observe certain rules. The structure of the sentence correction section constrains you to answer in accordance with the rules we must all observe without infecting your analysis with your own personal preferences.

Step 6: Guess

By this stage you surely will have been able to eliminate one or more of the choices as incorrect, so the odds favor a guess; and at this point, since you have followed the attack strategy as outlined, your choice can be nothing more than a guess:

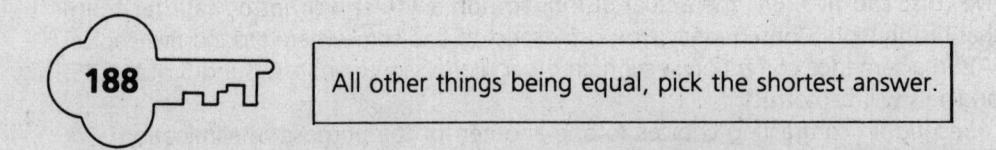

188 — All other things being equal, pick the shortest answer.

We stress that this is your last attempt—a guessing tactic. Remember that the section tests conciseness of expression and conciseness is often, though not necessarily indicated by the fewest words. At least Key 188 gives you a rule for making your final guess, and it has its basis in the structure of the exam.